"SCHOOL DAYS, SCHOOL DAYS, DEAR OLD GOLD MEDAL FLOUR DA

The COOKIE lover's COOKBOOK

Let them have another, Mother, they're pure NABISCO cookies

The *COOKIE* *lover's* ♥ COOKBOOK

COURAGE
BOOKS

AN IMPRINT OF RUNNING PRESS
PHILADELPHIA • LONDON

Credits

CLB 4961

This edition first published in 1998 in the United States by Courage Books.

© CLB International

A division of Quadrillion Publishing Ltd, Godalming, Surrey, GU7 1XW, England

Printed and bound in Singapore by Tien Wah Press

9 8 7 6 5 4 3 2 1

Digit on the right indicates the number of this printing

Library of Congress Cataloging-in-Publication Number 97-66745

ISBN 0-7624-0274-1

This book was designed and produced by CLB International
Godalming, Surrey, England, GU7 1XW

Contributor (pages 6–7): Phoebe Phillips

Consultant on cookie jars: Louise Messina Daking

Project management: Jo Richardson

Design: Liz Chidlow

Illustration: Philip Chidlow

Food photography: Amanda Heywood

Home economy: Elizabeth Wolf-Cohen

Antique photography: Geoff Daking; Neil Sutherland (see page 80 for full acknowledgments)

Picture research: Leora Kahn

Production: Ruth Arthur and Neil Randles

Color reproduction: HBM Print Ltd

Published by Courage Books
an imprint of Running Press Book Publishers
125 South Twenty-second Street
Philadelphia, Pennsylvania 19103-4399

Contents

Cookie History 6

Ingredients 8

Equipment 10

Techniques & Tips 12

Drop Cookies 14

Molded Cookies 24

Refrigerator & Rolled Cookies 36

Pressed & Piped Cookies 50

Bar Cookies 60

Special Cookies 70

Index & Acknowledgments 80

Cookie History

Origins and development of the world's favorite "little cakes"

Cookies: the word alone is enough to conjure up a plate piled high with rich chocolate and nut indulgences and a glass of cold milk. Alternatively, the word can denote a nice person, or it could mean the offer of a cup of tea and a slip of a lemon thin. "A fact of life" is a new meaning, when you say "that's the way the cookie crumbles." Or you can be international with a delicate French almond tuile or a crumbly triangle of Scottish shortbread.

More prosaically, the word has a rather straightforward provenance from the Dutch

A fanciful advertisement for Nabisco Sugar Wafers dating from 1904.

A printed tin in a Chinese bird pattern with a bamboo wrapped handle, c. 1910.

"koekje," meaning little cake. It came over with the first ships to New Amsterdam, and as far as the rest of the world is concerned, it never went home. Cookies are as American as apple pie, and yet in just the same way they are found the world over, in almost every culture and in every cuisine, and under a wide variety of names.

We can see from French and English recipes of the 14th century that the

NABISCO SUGAR WAFERS

knights and their aides adored sweetmeats, especially flat little cakes of golden saffron dough, their gilded tops melting gently in the mouth. Queen Elizabeth loved gingerbread cookies, spiced and decorated with pieces of candied fruit.

The Germans and Austrians bake some of the greatest cookies of all, redolent with ginger and cumin, poppy seed and nutmeg, and occasionally coated with dark, luscious chocolate. These were famous as Christmas treats, and they have been made since medieval times, when merchants traveled to the very furthest reaches of the known world to bring back rare spices.

But England became the heartland of the biscuit in the 19th century with relatively plain and delicately flavored cakes, baked to a particularly crisp texture which is the pride of manufacturers such as Peak Frean, Jacobs, or MacVitie. The biscuit became the natural partner of the English cup of tea, and since 1870, it has been sold in literally hundreds of mixtures and shapes.

For the collector, English biscuit barrels have that eccentric touch, in every medium from Georgian silver to Art Deco glass and richly colored litho-printed tins. Some were made in china or glass to match kitchen equipment, but the most intriguing are tins which date from 1880–1925, imitating jewelry boxes, horse carriages, Chinese bird-cages, castles, airplanes, even a pair of shoes. At Christmas, English biscuits are still sold as valued gifts in cheerfully decorated, air-tight tins, now usually simple boxes in shape, but which keep the contents crisp throughout the holiday.

Many other countries have strong traditions of making and baking little cakes. The Chinese have two or three favorite flat wafers, which are cut in rectangles or squares, plain or sandwiched with bean paste, or twisted to hold a little good luck sign, now adapted by America as Fortune Cookies.

Spanish and Portuguese bakers turn out platters of tiny delicacies for a late breakfast and for afternoon coffee; little biscuity tarts of lemon curd and honey, tiny filled cookies with coffee cream or praline icing, and pinwheel slices of vanilla and orange.

And finally, the American cookie—its name Dutch, its texture more cakey than its English sisters, its strong flavors with a heavy emphasis on chocolate and various nuts, its chewy, satisfying mouthful.

We have borrowed recipes from the world that yet remain uniquely American. There are cookies made in every region and every state, almost in every town and city. A Chicago cookbook from the 1920s offers 365 cookie recipes, one for every day in the year, and temptingly says it could have provided as many again.

So explore the great heritage of cookie-dom, with old-fashioned favorites and newly imaginative delicacies, plus a little history, too; Mexican wedding cookies, Austrian Chocolate Crescents, Italian Biscotti, Caribbean Lime Squares, and so on. These have all been adopted by American appetites, and they will add delicious (and fast-disappearing) variety to the contents of any cookie jar.

Phoebe Phillips

Art Deco glass biscuit jar c. 1920, no doubt for boudoir biscuits.

The manufacture of Peek, Freen, and Co.'s biscuits, from the London Illustrated News, *1874.*

A handmade wooden cookie board mold with a stylized rooster motif, dated c. 1800s.

Ingredients

A guide to selecting and using the best-quality items, for excellent results

Most cookies are made from a dough paste of butter, sugar, eggs, and flour in varying proportions. Because the true flavors of the ingredients really come through in cookies, it is important to use the best and freshest butter and eggs, pure vanilla and other extracts, fine spices, and the best chocolate.

Flour and grains

All-purpose flour is a blend of hard and soft wheats. Many people prefer unbleached flour since it is more natural and contains a higher proportion of vitamins, but both will give equally good results. Whole-wheat flour contains the wheat-germ and is heavier than all-purpose flour. Combine with white flour for the best results. Graham flour is slightly coarser ground whole-wheat flour. Different flours in various temperatures and levels of humidity will absorb more or less liquid.

Oats are often added to cookies for enhanced flavor, texture, fiber, and nutrients. Old-fashioned whole-grain rolled oats and quick oats (not instant oats) are best for baking. Cornstarch is a finely milled powder ground from corn kernels. It can help soften hard flours by replacing 1–2 tablespoons from 1 cup of all-purpose or hard-wheat flour in shortbreads or other delicate cookies.

Chemical raising agents

Baking soda combines with other acid ingredients such as buttermilk, sour cream, lemon juice, honey, or molasses to raise the dough. This action begins almost immediately, so any doughs containing baking soda should be baked as soon as they are mixed. Baking powder is a combination of baking soda and an acid salt, usually cream of tartar. Most baking powders provide two raising actions: the first when it comes into contact with the liquid ingredients, the second when the dough is heated. For this reason, the doughs should be mixed and baked immediately. Cream of tartar is used when beating egg whites for meringues and added to some icings to add stability.

Sugars and other sweeteners

Granulated sugar is the most commonly used sugar. However, in more delicate cookies it can show up as brown flakes. Superfine sugar is ideal for baking tender cookies since it dissolves and creams easily. Make your own by grinding

An advertisement from a culinary pamphlet published in 1924 featuring Karo syrup, used for flavoring cookies and cakes.

granulated sugar in a food proccessor using the metal blade. Confectioner's sugar is made by grinding granulated sugar and adding a small amount of cornstarch, to prevent caking. Light and dark brown sugars—granulated sugar with molasses added—add a dense, chewy texture to cookies.

Unsulfered molasses is a syrup made from boiled cane or beet sugar (dissolved in water) during the initial refining process. Black strap molasses is the very dark, strong residue from the third boiling. Maple syrup has a deep golden color and distinctive flavor. Use 100% real maple syrup for flavoring cookies. Corn syrup tends to absorb moisture, so is useful for keeping baked goods moist. Honey, either runny or set, provides moisture and texture in cookies.

Eggs and dairy products

Eggs provide texture, structure, flavor, and moisture in cookies. Unless specified, use large eggs in the recipes. Small babies, pregnant women, and the elderly should avoid eating raw or softly cooked eggs and meringues.

Unsalted butter is preferable for all baking. Because it contains no salt, which acts as a preservative, it tends to be fresher and also contains slightly less water and other impurities. Cream and milk come in many forms, usually according to their butterfat content. Unless specified in the recipes, use whole milk, or sour cream (about 18%) and yogurt.

A trade card for Hyler's Cocoa "... for purity and deliciousness of flavor unexcelled," from New York, dated 1899.

Chocolate and cocoa

Unsweetened chocolate is very dry and bitter, but has an intense chocolate flavor ideal for cookies and brownies. Semisweet chocolate contains more sugar than bittersweet. The latter will give a more intense chocolate flavor to most recipes. In the United States, dark chocolate must contain 34% solids, but best results are obtained with chocolate containing a minimum of 50% cocoa solids. Milk chocolate has a lower cocoa solids-content, and cannot be substituted for dark, bittersweet, or semisweet chocolate. Chocolate chips are designed to keep their shape when baked, although they can be melted. Choose a high-quality brand of white chocolate (confectionery coating). As with milk chocolate, it should be melted with care. Dutch-process cocoa powder has a reddish color and slightly milder flavor than the more common varieties.

Fruits and nuts

Dried fruits add flavor and texture to many cookies. Raisins, golden raisins, and currants are often

A bold and colorful trade card featuring Blue Valley Butter, produced in Chicago in the 1930s and 1940s.

used, but the range of dried fruits available is rapidly expanding. Try dried cranberries, sour cherries, blueberries, figs, apples, pears, and mango. Nuts almost always benefit from a light toasting to bring out their flavor.

Flavorings

Spices are found in almost every cookie. Cinnamon, nutmeg, and ginger are commonly used, but try cloves, mace, crushed cardamom seeds, and allspice as well. Grinding your own spices adds a more intense flavor; use an old coffee grinder (cleaned) for spice grinding, and grind your own nutmeg on the small side of a box grater.

Vanilla extract is the most convenient form of vanilla to use, but always use a pure extract. Vanilla beans are expensive but give wonderful results. Split a vanilla bean lengthwise with a sharp knife and scrape out the tiny black seeds with the tip of a knife.

Equipment

Making the best use of everyday and specialty items

Most cookies can be made using the basic equipment found in any ordinary working kitchen. However, be sure to read the recipe through before you start, so that you can be certain of having all the necessary equipment to hand, as well as all the ingredients required.

Measuring spoons and cups are essential for all home baking. Be sure to use measuring spoons and cups, not ordinary kitchen spoons and cups, for reliable results.

A conical molded cake of sugar, and a pair of nippers, used for breaking up sugar in the 18th and early 19th centuries.

Heatproof glass measuring cups should be used to measure liquids.

Most cookies can be made by hand—after all, they were all first made that way—but using an electric mixer, either a heavy-duty counter model or a hand-held type, saves both time and energy. For most cookies, a hand-mixer is ideal— it gives a feel of control over the dough. Some cookie doughs can be made with a food processor, although they are mostly used for chopping other ingredients such as nuts and chocolate—I find it a simply indispensable item.

Other general kitchenware useful in cookie-making are good nesting mixing bowls, sturdy wooden spoons for beating and creaming, and rubber spatulas and plastic dough scrapers for scraping out bowls and work surfaces. A selection of whisks and good knives is also essential. A pastry wheel is handy for cutting various cookies. Although a double boiler can be useful, a mixing bowl set over a saucepan makes a perfect substitute.

A rolling pin is essential for rolling out cookie doughs quickly and evenly. Many styles are available, some with handles and some without. My personal favorite is a 17½ x 1½-inch white Teflon rolling

A flour sifter, patented in 1922, with a turned wooden handle and a double lid (top and bottom) so that the flour can be sifted twice.

An unstamped cookie cutter made out of tin in the shape of a duck, dating back to the 19th century.

pin, which really does not stick (not often, anyway!). A long ruler is essential for measuring, and the straight edge is useful as a cutting guide.

Small ice cream scoops are ideal for forming drop cookies, and guarantee uniformly sized cookies. Cookie cutters of all sizes and shapes are available. Look for unusual ones in party stores and mail order catalogs. I have found a lovable lamb and a friendly looking dinosaur, as well as some charming Shaker people and gingergread children! A cookie press or cookie gun is essential for "spritz" (see page 54) and other molded cookies. They come with a variety of discs used to make different shapes. Other special molds, such as those used for making shortbread or "springerle," are available at specialty shops or by mail order.

Use heavy-gauge, flat, shiny aluminum baking sheets, at least 2-inches smaller than the inside of your oven, so that the heat can circulate evenly. Dark cookie sheets can absorb too much heat and cause the bottom of cookies to over-brown or cook too quickly. Very thin baking sheets may warp, distorting the shape of the cookies. Nonstick sheets are ideal for certain cookies, but may cause others to over-spread, so follow the instructions in the individual recipes. New cushionaire baking sheets with a thick insulated base are excellent, especially for thin cookies or meringues which tend to stick or over-brown on the bottom. It avoids using the cumbersome system of "double" baking sheets.

Other pans useful in making bar cookies, brownies, or even shortbread are a 9-inch jelly-roll pan, a 13 x 9-inch baking pan, a 15½ x 10½-inch jelly-roll pan, and 8- or 9-inch cake and tart pans, preferably with removable bottoms. If using a Pyrex baking dish, reduce the oven temperature by 25°F.

Wire cooling racks, pancake turners, and various metal palette knives are essential for cooking and removing cookies quickly and neatly from their baking sheets.

Pastry or decorating bags with a selection of tips can be used to pipe meringues, soft cookie doughs, and all kinds of icings.

Papers, foils, and plastics are really useful for cookie-making. Nonstick baking parchment is ideal for most jobs—although more expensive than other baking papers, it is well worth the extra cost. This special silicone-coated greaseproof paper can withstand direct contact with oven heat and so, unlike waxed paper, it will not burn. It is ideal for lining baking sheets for sticky cookies and meringues, lining cake pans, and making paper cones (see page 19, step 4). Waxed paper, a parafin-coated tissue paper, is inexpensive and ideal for wrapping doughs.

Cellophane is handy to have to transform special little bags of goodies

A multiple cake and cookie cutter with a number of motifs, including a cross, 6-pointed star, shamrock, and circle, made in the early 1980s in Hong Kong.

into attractive gifts with a happy sparkle.

Plastic wrap is a life-saver—ideal for wrapping and covering doughs and icings, it can be used to help roll out sticky doughs. Aluminum foil is also good for lining baking sheets and helps with easy clean-up. The most spectacular product yet is a nonstick Teflon®-coated material used by professionals, which creates a completely nonstick surface. It is available in sheets, which can be cut to fit baking sheets, pans, and griddles. Once used, it can simply be wiped off and used again. Look for it in speciality shops and mail order catalogs.

Two varieties of wooden corrugated cookie rollers, with separate turned handles and axle rods. These items both date from around the early 1900s.

Techniques & Tips

How to ensure excellent results every time you make or bake cookies

It is essential to master certain techniques for cookie-making. Most cookie doughs start by creaming the butter and sugar, then adding the liquid and dry ingredients. For the best results, all the ingredients should be at room temperature.

To cream the butter and sugar, use an electric mixer to combine the butter and sugar on low speeds. Increase the speed to medium and beat until the mixture lightens in color and texture and looks light and fluffy; this takes about 2 minutes. Alternatively, beat the butter first to soften it, then add the sugar and beat until it becomes light and fluffy. To beat whole eggs or yolks, usually with sugar, use an electric mixer on low speed to combine until blended, then increase the speed to medium and beat until the eggs are thickened and lightened in texture—from 2–5 minutes, depending on the recipe.

To beat egg whites, be sure all the equipment is clean and grease-free. Use an electric mixer on low speed and beat until the whites are frothy. Add the cream of tartar or salt, if the recipe directs, and increase the speed to medium-high until soft peaks form. For stiff peaks, beat a little longer until a sharp peak forms when the beater is lifted out. If adding sugar for meringues, it should be added gradually once the soft peaks form.

To fold in beaten egg whites or other ingredients without deflating a mixture, use a large metal kitchen spoon or rubber spatula to gently cut down through the center and along the side of the bowl in a circular movement. This method combines the mixtures, while retaining as much air as possible.

To melt chocolate, chop it and put in the top of a double boiler set over the bottom pan of barely simmering water. Stir until melted and smooth. Alternatively, put the chocolate in a heatproof bowl set over a saucepan of barely simmering water. It is essential that no liquid comes into contact with the chocolate, since it may cause it to seize and harden. I prefer to melt chocolate in the microwave, athough great care must be taken not to overheat and burn it. Microwave 4 ounces of chopped dark chocolate on medium power (50%) for about 2 minutes, then remove and stir until smooth. Decrease the power to low (30%) for milk and white chocolate. If not completely melted, microwave at 5–10 second intervals until completely melted and smooth.

Grind nuts in a food processor fitted with the metal blade using the pulse action until fine crumbs form. If there is sugar or flour in the recipe, add a tablespoon with the nuts to prevent them from being over-processed.

TIPS FOR PERFECT COOKIE-BAKING

Whatever the method used for making them, cookie doughs contain a high percentage of fat and sugar. Therefore, they require little baking and tend to burn easily. Follow the tips on the opposite page for best results.

• Before you start, read the recipe and assemble everything you will need. Be sure the ingredients are at room temperature (unless otherwise stated)—adding cold eggs to a butter mixture can cause it to curdle.

• Measure and sift together the dry ingredients before starting. This ensures any spices and leaveners are well blended and the mixture is well aerated.

• Measure leaveners by a level, not heaped, measuring spoon, and liquids in a glass measuring cup at eye level.

• Stir in any small chopped ingredients by hand to be sure they are evenly distributed.

• Eggs should be beaten lightly before being gradually added to a creamed butter-sugar mixture, to avoid curdling. If the mixture does curdle, stir in a tablespoon of the measured dry ingredients, then continue.

• Cut butter into small pieces and spread out on a plate to bring it to room temperature more quickly, or microwave on high (full power) at 2–3 second intervals; do not allow it to melt.

• Most butter-rich cookie doughs don't require greased baking sheets, but a thin layer of vegetable shortening (butter can burn) can be used as a precaution. I prefer a baking/cooking vegetable oil spray for the lightest of coatings. Otherwise, use a pastry brush for a light, even coating of oil, or line with foil, nonstick baking parchment, or as directed.

• Be sure the oven is preheated to the temperature required.

• Arrange cookies evenly spaced on baking sheets, trying not to leave any large empty areas. Leave enough room for cookies to spread. Chilling the dough before arranging on baking sheets helps prevent spreading.

• Try to bake cookies one sheet at a time in the center of the oven so that the air circulates evenly. Otherwise, rotate the baking sheets from the bottom shelf to the top shelf and from back to front halfway through the cooking time.

• Never use a hot baking sheet. For quick cooling, run the back of a baking sheet under cold water, wipe dry, and regrease. Alternatively, arrange cookies on sheets of foil or baking parchment cut to fit the baking sheets. As soon as baked cookies are removed from the baking sheet, slide a prepared sheet of foil or parchment onto the baking sheet and bake immediately.

• Baking times can vary. Begin by testing at the minimum time. Let the cookies cool completely in a single layer on a wire rack before storing. Use a timer to avoid overbaking. Because they are relatively thin, cookies will continue to bake after removing from the oven. Allow them to firm slightly before removing from the baking sheet.

• Store most cookies in airtight containers or tins. Store different kinds separately since the flavors might blend, or moist cookies might soften crisp ones.

• Separate delicate or sticky cookies with waxed paper or foil. To recrisp, reheat for 3–5 minutes on a baking sheet in a 300°F oven.

• Refrigerator cookie dough can be made ahead and then frozen. Thaw in the refrigerator until just soft enough to slice.

Drop Cookies

Death by Chocolate

Makes about 2 dozen large cookies

These cookies are large and flat, crisp on the edge, soft in the center, and filled with chocolate.

Vegetable oil spray or vegetable oil, for greasing

9 ounces bittersweet or semisweet chocolate, chopped

¾ cup (1½ sticks) unsalted butter, cut into pieces

3 eggs

¾ cup superfine sugar

⅓ cup packed brown sugar

2 teaspoons vanilla extract

½ cup all-purpose flour

6 tablespoons cocoa powder, sifted

1½ teaspoons baking powder

¼ teaspoon salt

9 ounces semisweet chocolate, chopped into ¼-inch pieces (about 1½ cups) or 1½ cups semisweet chocolate chips

6 ounces chocolate, chopped into ¼-inch pieces

6 ounces white chocolate, chopped into ¼-inch pieces

1½ cups pecans or walnuts, toasted and chopped

1. Preheat the oven to 325°F. Lightly spray or grease 2 large baking sheets. In a medium saucepan over low heat, melt the chocolate and butter, stirring frequently until smooth. Set aside to cool slightly.

2. In a large bowl, using an electric mixer, beat the eggs and sugars for 2–3 minutes on low speed, until thick and pale. Gradually beat in the melted chocolate and vanilla extract until well blended. In a small bowl, stir together the flour, cocoa powder, baking powder, and salt until blended, then gently stir into chocolate mixture. Stir in the chocolate pieces and nuts.

3. Drop heaping tablespoonfuls of the mixture at least 4 inches apart onto the baking sheets. Wet the bottom of a drinking glass and flatten each dough round slightly, to make each about 3 inches round; you will only fit 4–6 cookies on each sheet. Bake for 10 minutes, until the tops are cracked and shiny. Do not overbake or the cookies will break when removed from the baking sheet.

4. Remove the baking sheets to wire racks to cool slightly and set. Using a metal pancake turner or thin-bladed metal spatula, carefully remove each cookie to wire racks to cool completely. Repeat with the remaining cooking dough. Store in an airtight container.

Fruit 'n' Nut Oatmeal Cookies

Makes about 3 dozen cookies

BE SURE TO USE OLD-FASHIONED ROLLED OATS OR QUICK-COOKING OATMEAL IN THESE CHEWY COOKIES.

3 cups raisins

1 cup dried cranberries or cherries

1 cup boiling water

Vegetable oil spray or vegetable oil, for greasing

¾ cup (1½ sticks) unsalted butter, softened

1½ cups packed light brown sugar

2 eggs, lightly beaten

1½ teaspoons vanilla extract

2½ cups all-purpose flour

½ teaspoon baking powder

1½ teaspoons baking soda

½ teaspoon salt

2 teaspoons ground cinnamon

1 teaspoon ground ginger

½ teaspoon ground allspice

2 cups old-fashioned (rolled) oats

2 cups chopped walnuts or pecans, lightly toasted

1½ cups pitted prunes, chopped

1 cup chopped pitted dates

1. In a small bowl, combine the dried fruit. Pour over the boiling water and allow to stand, covered, for ¼ hour, stirring occasionally. Drain, reserving ⅓ cup of the soaking liquid, and set aside.

2. Preheat the oven to 400°F. Lightly spray or grease 2 large baking sheets. In a large bowl, using an electric mixer, beat the butter until creamy. Add the sugar and continue beating for about 2 minutes, until light and fluffy. Slowly beat in the eggs and vanilla extract.

3. Sift the flour, baking powder, baking soda, salt, cinnamon, ginger, and allspice into a large bowl. Add the butter mixture alternately with the reserved soaking liquid, mixing well until blended. Stir in the oats, walnuts or pecans, prunes, dates, and soaked raisins.

4. Drop heaping tablespoonfuls of the mixture onto the baking sheets at least 3 inches apart. Flatten slightly with the back of a moistened spoon. Bake for 6–8 minutes, until golden and set. Remove the baking sheets to wire racks to cool slightly. Using a metal pancake turner, transfer the cookies to wire racks to cool completely. Repeat with the remaining cookie dough. Store the cookies in an airtight container.

This charming Raggedy Ann cookie jar was made by The Nelson McCoy Company.

New Wave Peanut Butter Cookies

Makes 18 cookies

Peanut butter cookies have been traditional for decades, but these have extra peanuts and white chocolate.

1 cup freshly shelled peanuts

Vegetable oil spray or vegetable oil, for greasing

1 cup all-purpose flour

½ teaspoon baking soda

¼ teaspoon salt

½ cup chunky peanut butter

½ cup (1 stick) unsalted butter, softened

½ cup packed light brown sugar

2 tablespoons sugar

1 egg, lightly beaten

1 teaspoon vanilla extract

6 ounces white chocolate chips or white chocolate, coarsely chopped

1. Put the peanuts in a medium skillet or frying pan, and toast over medium-low heat for about 5 minutes, until golden and fragrant, stirring frequently. Pour the nuts onto a plate and leave to cool.

2. Preheat the oven to 375°F. Lightly spray or grease 2 large baking sheets. Sift the flour, baking soda, and salt into a medium bowl. In a large bowl, using an electric mixer, beat the peanut butter, butter, and sugars together for 2–3 minutes, until light and fluffy. Gradually add the egg and continue beating for 2 minutes more. Beat in the vanilla extract. Stir in the flour mixture until blended, then the chocolate and peanuts.

3. Drop heaping tablespoonfuls of the mixture at least 2 inches apart onto the baking sheets.

Flatten slightly with the back of a moistened spoon. Bake for 10 minutes, until golden brown. Do not overbake.

4. Remove the baking sheets to wire racks to cool for 5 minutes. Transfer each cookie to wire racks to cool completely. Store in an airtight container.

Cream Cheese Macadamia Drops with White Chocolate

Makes about 20 cookies

½ cup (1 stick) unsalted butter, softened

8 ounces cream cheese, softened

¼ cup packed light brown sugar

Grated zest of 1 lemon

1½ teaspoons vanilla extract

1½ cups all-purpose flour

2 teaspoons baking powder

1 cup coarsely chopped unsalted macadamia nuts

4 ounces white chocolate, coarsely chopped

Vegetable oil spray or vegetable oil, for greasing

6 ounces white chocolate, melted (optional)

THE MACADAMIA NUT IS RICH AND CREAMY, AND GOES PERFECTLY WITH THE CREAM CHEESE BASE AND WHITE CHOCOLATE CHUNKS.

1. In a large bowl, using an electric mixer, beat the butter and cream cheese for 1–2 minutes, until creamy, scraping the bowl occasionally. Add the sugar and continue beating for 1–2 minutes more, until light and fluffy. Beat in the lemon zest and vanilla extract.

2. Sift the flour and baking powder into a bowl, and stir into the cream cheese mixture. Stir in the chopped nuts and chocolate. Chill the dough for about half an hour, until firm.

3. Preheat the oven to 400°F. Lightly spray or grease 2 large baking sheets. Drop heaping teaspoonfuls of the mixture 2 inches apart onto the baking sheets, and flatten slightly. Bake for 8–10 minutes, until puffed and golden. Remove the baking sheets to wire racks to cool for about 5 minutes, then transfer the cookies to wire racks to cool completely. Repeat with the remaining mixture.

This advertisement jar for Nestlé's Toll House cookies is a highly collectable item, made by the Abingdon Pottery Company, Illinois.

4. If you like, make a cone for piping the chocolate. Fold a square of waxed paper in half to form a triangle. With the triangle point facing you, fold the left corner down to the center. Fold the right corner down and wrap around the folded left corner. Fill the cone with the chocolate, then fold the top edges over to enclose it. Snip off the tip to make a hole ⅛-inch in diameter. Pipe over the cookies in a zig-zag pattern and allow to set.

Chocolate Turtles

Makes about 2 dozen cookies

THIS OLD-TIME FAVORITE IS ENRICHED WITH EXTRA CHOCOLATE AND NUTS. THE PECANS ARE MEANT TO RESEMBLE THE HEAD, ARMS, AND LEGS OF THE TURTLE.

12 ounces semisweet chocolate, chopped

3 ounces (3 squares) unsweetened chocolate, chopped

¼ cup (½ stick) unsalted butter, cut into pieces

1½ cups sugar

4 eggs, lightly beaten

1 teaspoon vanilla extract

½ cup all-purpose flour

1 tablespoon instant espresso powder

½ teaspoon baking powder

¼ teaspoon salt

2 cups coarsely chopped pecans or walnuts

2 cups semisweet chocolate chips

2 cups pecan halves, to decorate

1. Preheat the oven to 350°F. Line 2 large baking sheets with foil or nonstick baking parchment. In a medium saucepan over medium-low heat, melt the chocolates with the butter until smooth, stirring frequently. Add half the sugar and stir until dissolved. Remove from the heat and beat in the eggs, remaining sugar, and vanilla extract.

2. Sift together the flour, espresso powder, baking powder, and salt into a medium bowl. Stir into the chocolate mixture until blended, then stir in the chopped nuts and chocolate chips.

3. Using an ice cream scoop or ¼-cup measure, drop dough onto the baking sheets at least 3 inches apart, and flatten slightly. Insert 5 pecans into the edge of each cookie to represent the head and legs of a turtle. Bake, one sheet at a time, in the center of the oven, for about 10 minutes, just until the surface of the cookies begins to split. Do not overbake; the cookies should be soft in the center.

4. Remove the baking sheets to wire racks to cool slightly. Gently peel off the foil or paper and cool completely. Repeat with the remaining cookie dough and nuts. Store in an airtight container.

Nursery Rhyme characters feature widely in the designs for cookie jars. This Humpty Dumpty is a lovely example, made by Purinton.

DIAMOND BRAND WALNUTS

An advertisement for Diamond Brand Walnuts taken from a culinary pamphlet dating back to the 1930s and 1940s in California.

Chocolate Nut Crackles

Makes about 20 cookies

THESE CHOCOLATE-COFFEE-NUT COOKIES ARE BIG, RICH, AND INTENSELY FLAVORED. DO NOT OVERBAKE OR THEY WILL BE DRY.

9 ounces (9 squares) bittersweet or semisweet chocolate

3 ounces (3 squares) unsweetened chocolate, chopped

½ cup (1 stick) plus 1 tablespoon butter, softened

6 tablespoons all-purpose flour

½ teaspoon baking powder

3 eggs

1 cup sugar

1 tablespoon instant espresso powder

1 tablespoon vanilla extract

1½ cups pecans, coarsely chopped

1½ cups hazelnuts, coarsely chopped

1½ cups semisweet chocolate chips

1. In a medium saucepan over low heat, melt the chocolates with the butter until smooth, stirring frequently. Set aside to cool. Sift the flour and baking powder into a small bowl and set aside.

2. Preheat the oven to 325°F. In a large bowl, using an electric mixer, beat the eggs with the sugar for about 2 minutes, until light and fluffy. Beat in the melted chocolate mixture, then the espresso powder and vanilla extract until well blended. Add the flour mixture and beat until just combined, then stir in the nuts and chocolate chips.

3. Using a medium ice cream scoop or ½-cup measure, scoop out the cookie dough and arrange in mounds at least 3 inches apart on large ungreased baking sheets. Bake each sheet, one at a time, for about 25 minutes, until the cookie tops just begin to crack. Remove the baking sheet to a wire rack and cool for 5 minutes. Transfer cookies to a wire rack to cool completely. Continue baking in batches.

Lacy Oatmeal Wafers

Makes about 2 dozen cookies

1½ cups quick-cooking rolled oats

1 cup packed light brown sugar

½ cup superfine sugar

2 tablespoons all-purpose flour

¼ teaspoon salt

⅔ cup (1 stick) plus 2⅔ tablespoons unsalted butter, melted

1 egg, lightly beaten

1 teaspoon vanilla extract

½ cup mini chocolate chips (optional)

1. Preheat the oven to 350°F. In a large bowl, stir together the oats, sugars, flour, and salt. Make a well in the center and add the melted butter, egg, and vanilla. Stir until well blended and a soft batter-like dough forms. Stir in the chocolate chips, if using.

2. Drop teaspoonfuls of the mixture 2½ inches apart onto ungreased baking sheets. Bake for 3–5 minutes, until the edges are lightly brown and the centers are bubbling; the cookies will spread to large discs. Remove the baking sheets to wire racks to cool slightly.

3. When the edges of the cookies are firm enough to lift, use a thin-bladed metal spatula to remove to wire racks to cool. Store in airtight containers with waxed paper between each layer of cookies.

Coconut Macaroons

Makes about 2 dozen cookies

BECAUSE THEY CONTAIN NO FLOUR, THESE COOKIES WERE ALWAYS MADE AT PASSOVER BY MY FRIEND BARBARA.

3 cups sweetened, shredded coconut

1 cup unsalted macadamia nuts, chopped

Vegetable oil spray or vegetable oil, for greasing

⅔ cup sweetened condensed milk

1 teaspoon vanilla extract

2 egg whites

Pinch of salt

1. Preheat the oven to 350°F. Place the shredded coconut onto a large baking sheet and the macadamia nuts onto another baking sheet. Toast for 7–10 minutes, until lightly golden, stirring and shaking each sheet freqently. Pour the coconut onto a plate and the nuts onto another plate to cool completely.

2. Line 2 large baking sheets with nonstick baking parchment paper, and spray or very lightly grease with oil. In a large bowl, stir together the condensed milk, vanilla extract, shredded coconut, and macadamia nuts until well blended.

3. In a medium bowl, using an electric mixer on medium speed, beat the egg whites until foamy. Add the salt and increase the mixer speed to high. Continue beating until the whites are stiff but not dry. Fold the whites into the coconut mixture. Drop rounded tablespoonfuls onto the baking sheets, and shape each one into a cone. Bake for 10–12 minutes, until golden around the edges. Remove the baking sheets to wire racks to cool completely, then gently peel off the paper.

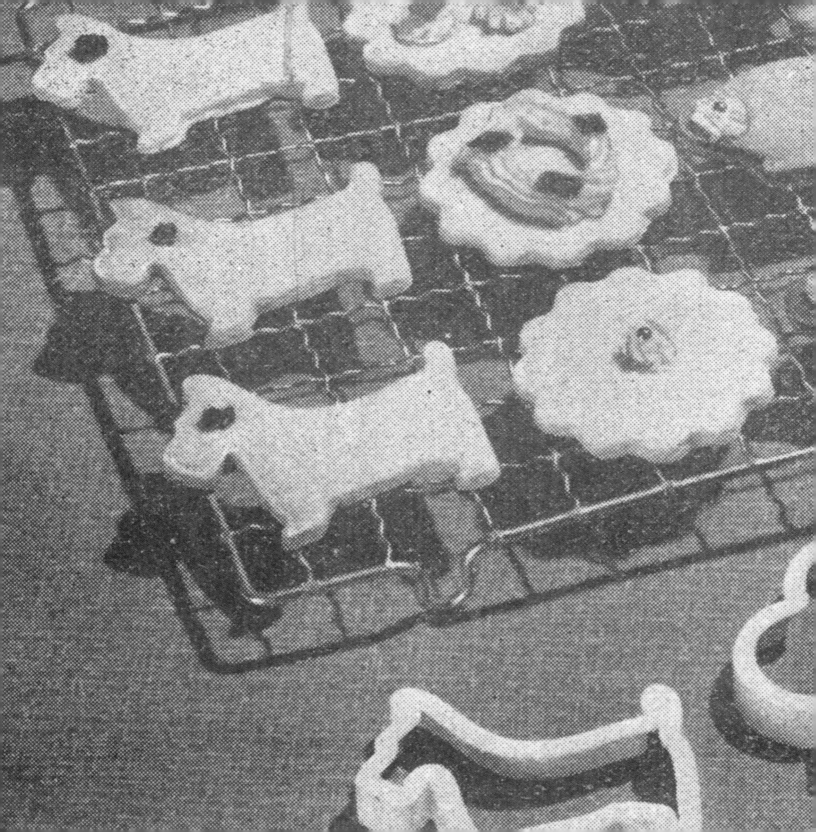

Molded Cookies

Pine Nut Macaroons

Makes about 2 dozen cookies

THESE DELICIOUS CHEWY COOKIES ARE FULL OF ALMOND-PINE NUT FLAVORS. TRY MAKING A SANDWICH COOKIE USING A LITTLE APRICOT JAM, AS THEY DO IN ITALY.

3 tablespoons dried currants

3 tablespoons Marsala or sweet wine

¾ cup slivered blanched almonds, lightly toasted

½ cup pine nuts, toasted

½ cup superfine sugar

1 tablespoon all-purpose flour

1 egg white

¼ teaspoon almond extract

1 cup pine nuts

1. Preheat the oven to 350°F. Line a large baking sheet with foil (shiny side up) or nonstick baking parchment. In a small bowl, combine the currants and Marsala or sweet wine, and heat in a microwave oven on High (100% power) for 30–60 seconds. Allow to stand for 3–5 minutes, until the liquid is absorbed, then cool.

Hand-made cookie wooden board mold with a pig motif dating from around the 1800s.

2. In a food processor, using the metal blade, process the toasted almonds and pine nuts, sugar, and flour until finely ground. Add the egg white and almond extract, and using the pulse button, process until the mixture forms a dough. Turn into a bowl and stir in the currants.

3. Put the untoasted pine nuts into a medium bowl or pie plate. Wet your hands and using a teaspoon to scoop out the dough, shape it into ¾-inch balls. Roll the balls in the pine nuts, pressing lightly to cover completely. Place the balls 1½ inches apart onto the baking sheet. Flatten slightly to make a disc shape.

4. Bake the cookies for 12–15 minutes, until the pine nuts are golden, rotating the baking sheet front to back halfway through cooking. Remove to a wire rack to cool for 2–3 minutes. Remove the cookies to a wire rack to cool completely.

Store in an airtight container.

Peanut Butter Cookie-Cups

Makes about 2 dozen cookies

THE COMBINATION OF CHOCOLATE AND PEANUT BUTTER IS A POPULAR ONE. THIS VERY PEANUTY COOKIE, FILLED WITH A CREAMY CHOCOLATE GANACHE SWIRL, IS HEAVENLY!

PEANUT-BUTTER COOKIE
1 cup all-purpose flour
1 teaspoon baking powder
¼ teaspoon salt
½ cup (1 stick) unsalted butter, softened
½ cup packed light brown sugar
¼ cup sugar

1 cup smooth peanut butter
1 egg
1 teaspoon vanilla extract

CHOCOLATE FILLING
12 ounces semisweet or bittersweet chocolate, chopped
6 tablespoons (¾ stick) unsalted butter, softened

1. Sift the flour, baking powder, and salt into a small bowl. In a large mixing bowl, using an electric mixer, beat the butter for 1 minute, until creamy. Add the sugars and continue beating until the mixture is light and fluffy. Add the peanut butter in 3 batches, beating well after each addition, until the mixture is well blended. Beat in the egg and vanilla extract. Stir in the flour mixture until just blended. Refrigerate the dough for about 1 hour, until chilled.

2. Preheat the oven to 375°F. Using a tablespoon, scoop out the mixture, and using slightly moistened hands, roll between your palms to form l-inch balls. Place the balls 1½ inches apart on 2 large, ungreased baking sheets. Using a finger or the handle of a wooden spoon, press down into the center of each ball to make a deep hole. Bake for 10–12 minutes, until just set and golden, rotating the baking sheets from the top to the bottom shelf and from front to back halfway through the cooking time.

3. Remove the baking sheets to wire racks to cool for 2–3 minutes, until the cookies are firm enough to move. Using a metal pancake turner, transfer to a wire rack to cool. Repeat with the remaining mixture.

4. When the cookies are completely cooled, put the chocolate into a medium bowl. Set the bowl over a saucepan of just simmering water and heat until the chocolate is melted and smooth, stirring frequently. Remove from the heat and cool slightly. Gently beat in the butter until the mixture just thickens. Spoon into a decorating bag fitted with a medium star tip. Pipe a small amount of chocolate ganache into the center of each cookie and allow to set until firm. Store in airtight containers with waxed paper between the layers.

Chocolate-Dipped Hazelnut Crescents

Makes about 36 cookies

AUSTRIAN CRESCENTS ARE GENERALLY MADE WITH GROUND ALMONDS. THIS VARIETY USES HAZELNUTS, WHICH GO BEAUTIFULLY WITH CHOCOLATE.

1 cup all-purpose flour
1 cup cake flour
¼ teaspoon salt
⅔ cup hazelnuts, toasted until golden
1 cup (2 sticks) unsalted butter, softened
⅓ cup superfine sugar

1 tablespoon hazelnut or almond flavor liqueur
1 teaspoon vanilla extract
Confectioner's sugar for dusting
6 ounces semisweet chocolate, melted, for dipping

1. Sift the flours and salt into a medium bowl, and stir together to mix well.

2. Preheat the oven to 325°F. In a food processor,

A levered nutcracker, made from cast iron in around 1870 to 1880.

using the metal blade, process the toasted hazelnuts until fine crumbs form; the nuts should be finely chopped but not ground.

3. In a large bowl, using an electric mixer, beat the butter for about 1 minute, until creamy. Add the sugar and beat for 1–2 minutes, until the mixture is light and fluffy. Beat in the liqueur and vanilla extract. Gently stir in the flour mixture until just blended, then fold in the finely chopped hazelnuts.

4. With lightly floured hands, form the dough into 1½ inch balls, placing them on a large baking sheet until all the dough is used. Roll each ball into a 2 x ½-inch crescent shape, and place 2 inches apart on another large, ungreased baking sheet. Bake for 20–25 minutes, until the edges are set and the cookies are lightly golden, rotating the baking sheet from front to back halfway through the cooking time. Remove the baking sheet to a wire rack to cool for 10 minutes. Remove each cookie to a wire rack to cool. Repeat with the remaining crescents until they are all baked.

This Smiley Pig cookie jar was one of Shawnee's most popular designs. The company created many quality jars in Ohio in the 1930s and 1940s.

5. Arrange the crescents side by side on a wire rack set over a baking sheet to catch drips, then dust them with confectioner's sugar. Using kitchen tongs or fingers, dip half of each cookie into melted chocolate, or spoon a "strip" of chocolate over the center. Place on waxed paper-lined baking sheets and refrigerate for 10–15 minutes, until set. Store in an airtight container with waxed paper between the layers.

Cookie Jar Gingersnaps

Makes about 4 dozen cookies

2 cups all-purpose flour

1 tablespoon ground ginger

2 teaspoons baking soda

1½ teaspoons ground cinnamon

½ teaspoon ground cloves

½ teaspoon salt

¾ cup white vegetable shortening

1 cup sugar

1 egg, lightly beaten

¼ cup molasses

Sugar, for rolling

1. Preheat the oven to 350°F. Sift the flour, ginger, baking soda, cinnamon, ground cloves, and salt into a medium bowl.

2. In a large bowl, using an electric mixer, beat the shortening for 1 minute, until soft. Gradually add the sugar and continue beating until the mixture is light and fluffy. Beat in the egg and molasses, then stir in the flour mixture until throughly blended.

3. Pour the sugar into a medium bowl. Using a heaped teaspoon, scoop out the mixture. Using your palms, roll into ¾-inch balls and roll in the sugar. Place 2 inches apart on ungreased baking sheets.

4. Bake for about 10 minutes, until the cookies are slightly rounded and the tops are lightly browned and crackled. Remove the baking sheets to wire racks to cool. Remove the cookies to wire racks to cool completely. Store in an airtight container.

Honey and Lemon Madeleines

Makes about 1 dozen cookies

1 cup plus 1 tablespoon all-purpose flour, sifted

1 teaspoon baking powder

Butter, for greasing

2 eggs

⅓ cup honey

¼ cup superfine sugar

Grated zest of 1 large lemon

1 tablespoon lemon juice

½ teaspoon vanilla extract

6 tablespoons (¾ stick) unsalted butter, melted and cooled

Confectioner's sugar, for dusting

1. Preheat the oven to 375°F. Sift the flour and baking powder into a small bowl. Lightly butter a 12-cup madeleine mold. In a large bowl, using an electric mixer, beat the eggs, honey, and sugar for 5–7 minutes, until light and pale and a slowly falling ribbon forms when the beaters are lifted from the bowl. Gently fold in the lemon zest and juice and the vanilla extract.

2. Beginning and ending with the flour, alternately gently fold in the flour and melted butter in 4 or 5 batches. Allow the batter to rest for 10 minutes, then spoon into the molds, almost filling them.

3. Bake for 10–12 minutes, until the tops spring back when gently pressed, rotating the molds from front to back three-quarters through cooking. Remove and immediately unmold onto a wire rack to cool. Dust with confectioner's sugar.

Mexican Wedding Cakes

Makes about 3 dozen cookies

Mexican Wedding Cakes are a traditional cookie, so-called because they resemble wedding bells, thickly dusted with confectioner's sugar.

¾ cup pecan or walnut halves

¾ cup confectioner's sugar

½ teaspoon ground cinnamon

1 cup (2 sticks) butter, cut into pieces, softened

1 teaspoon vanilla extract

2 cups all-purpose flour

¼ teaspoon salt

Confectioner's sugar, for rolling

1. Preheat the oven to 375°F. Put the pecans or walnuts on a baking sheet and toast for 7–10 minutes, until golden, stirring and shaking the baking sheet occasionally. Pour onto a plate to cool completely. Turn off the oven.

2. In a food processor, using the metal blade, process the toasted pecans or walnuts with the confectioner's sugar and cinnamon until fine crumbs form. Add the butter and process until creamy and smooth, scraping the side of the bowl once. Add the vanilla extract and pulse to blend. Add the flour and salt, and using the pulse action, process until the mixture begins to stick together and form a soft dough. Scrape into a bowl, cover, and refrigerate for 1–2 hours, until firm.

3. Preheat the oven to 375°F. Using a small scoop or tablespoon and lightly floured hands, shape the dough into l-inch balls, rolling them between your palms. Place the balls 1½ inches apart on 2 large ungreased baking sheets. Bake for about 10 minutes, until the cookies are barely golden, rotating the baking sheets from the top to the bottom shelf and from front to back halfway through the cooking time. Remove the baking sheets to wire racks to cool for 2 minutes.

4. Put about 1 cup of confectioner's sugar into a medium bowl. While the cookies are still warm, drop them into the bowl a few at a time and roll to coat well. Transfer to wire racks to cool completely. Repeat with the remaining cookie dough. Roll again in confectioner's sugar before storing in airtight containers.

Almond and Ginger Biscotti

Makes about 4 dozen cookies

DELICIOUS WITH ESPRESSO COFFEE OR DIPPED IN SWEET ITALIAN WINE—*VIN SAUTO*—THESE DRY CRUNCHY BISCUITS ARE AN ITALIAN VERSION OF GERMAN ALMOND BREAD.

2½ cups all-purpose flour

½ cup finely ground almonds

1 teaspoon baking soda

½ teaspoon salt

½ teaspoon allspice

1 teaspoon ground ginger

1½ cups blanched almonds, toasted and coarsely chopped

¾ cup pine nuts, toasted

2 eggs

1 cup superfine sugar

½ cup packed light brown sugar

¼ cup (½ stick) unsalted butter, melted and cooled

1½ teaspoon almond or vanilla extract

Grated zest of 1 lemon

2 tablespoons (1 ounce) chopped candied ginger *

Milk, for glazing

1. Preheat the oven to 375°F. Line a large baking sheet with heavy-duty foil. In a large bowl, combine the flour, ground almonds, baking soda, salt, allspice, ground ginger, chopped almonds, and pine nuts. In another bowl, whisk the eggs until foamy, then whisk in the sugars, melted butter, almond or vanilla extract, lemon zest, and ginger. Gradually stir the flour mixture into the egg mixture until a dough forms.

2. Turn out onto a lightly floured surface and knead lightly, just until the nuts are evenly distributed through the dough. Divide the dough in half and form into 2 even log shapes about 3-inches wide and 10-inches long.

3. Using a thin-bladed metal spatula, transfer each log to the baking sheet, setting 2–3 inches apart. Lightly brush each log with a little milk and bake for about 25 minutes, until golden and a toothpick comes out clean when inserted in the center, rotating the baking sheet from front to back halfway through the cooking time. Remove the baking sheet to a wire rack to cool slightly for about 10 minutes. Reduce the oven temperature to 325°F.

4. While the logs are still warm and soft, with a sharp knife, score each log crosswise into ½-inch wide slices. Transfer to a work surface and allow to cool for a further 5 minutes. Using a sharp serrated knife, carefully cut through the scored slices and arrange, cut sides down, on a baking sheet (you may need another large baking sheet at this point). Bake the biscotti for about 20 minutes, until golden and crisp, turning once halfway through the cooking time.

5. Remove the biscotti to wire racks to cool completely. Allow them to stand for 2–3 hours, until crisp, then store in airtight containers or jars.

* Candied ginger is available in some large supermarkets and specialty stores.

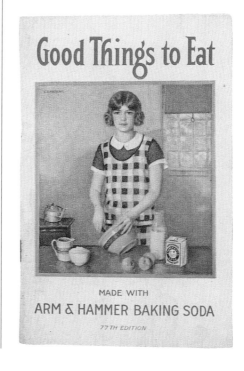

Good Things to Eat

MADE WITH
ARM & HAMMER BAKING SODA
77TH EDITION

Peppermint Cookie Canes

Makes about 2 dozen cookies

THIS BASIC COOKIE DOUGH IS TINTED WITH FOOD COLORING BEFORE BEING FORMED INTO CANDY CANE SHAPES. TIE WITH A RIBBON AND USE AS CHRISTMAS DECORATIONS.

2½ cups all-purpose flour

¼ teaspoon salt

1 cup (2 sticks) unsalted butter, softened

1 cup confectioner's sugar, sifted

1 egg, lightly beaten

½ teaspoon vanilla extract

½ teaspoon peppermint extract

¼ teaspoon red food coloring, optional

¼ cup crushed peppermint candy

A 198-pound flour bag from J. H. Gaebe & Co, Addieville, Illinois, boasting the name "Perfection." This quality flour was made from selected red winter wheat, as the label states.

1. Sift the flour and salt into a medium bowl. In a large bowl, using an electric mixer, beat the butter for about 30 seconds, until creamy. Gradually add the sugar and beat for 1–2 minutes, until light and fluffy. Beat in the egg and the vanilla and peppermint extracts, until blended. With the mixer on low speed, gradually beat in the flour.

2. Remove half the dough and wrap tightly in a piece of plastic wrap. Add the red food coloring and crushed peppermint candy to the remaining dough and beat until thoroughly mixed. Wrap tightly in plastic wrap and refrigerate both doughs for about 1 hour, until firm.

3. Preheat the oven to 350°F. Line 2 large baking sheets with foil or nonstick baking parchment. To form the cookies, use a teaspoon to scoop a piece of plain dough, then roll into a rope shape 4–6 inches long. Repeat with the red-colored dough, then twist the ropes together and bend the top end to make a cane shape. Repeat with the remaining doughs and set the canes about 2 inches apart on the baking sheets.

This is a cookie jar of legendary popularity— Little Red Riding Hood of nursery rhyme fame. Hull, the manufacturers, made many different versions of this ever-enduring jar.

4. Bake the canes for 8–10 minutes, until firm; do not allow them to brown or the color effect will not show sufficiently. Remove the baking sheets to wire racks to cool slightly for a few minutes. Transfer the canes to wire racks to cool completely. Store in airtight containers.

Refrigerator & Rolled Cookies

Gingery Chocolate Cookies

Makes about 3 dozen cookies

USING FRESH GINGERROOT GIVES THESE COOKIES A DEFINITE ZING. THE DOUGH CAN BE FROZEN FOR UP TO 2 MONTHS, THEN SLICED AND BAKED WITHOUT DEFROSTING.

2–3 inch piece of fresh gingerroot, peeled

2½ cups all-purpose flour

2 tablespoons unsweetened cocoa powder (preferably Dutch-processed)

½ teaspoon ground ginger

½ teaspoon salt

¼ teaspoon finely ground black pepper

1 cup (2 sticks) unsalted butter, softened

1 cup packed dark brown sugar

2 egg yolks

2 teaspoons vanilla extract

12 ounces bittersweet or semisweet chocolate, chopped

Chopped candied ginger, to decorate

1. Grate the piece of gingerroot against the small round holes of a box grater and set aside. Sift the flour, cocoa powder, ground ginger, salt, and pepper into a medium bowl.

2. In a large bowl, using an electric mixer, beat the butter for 30 seconds, until creamy. Add the brown sugar and continue beating for 1–2 minutes, until light and fluffy. Beat in the egg yolks and vanilla extract until the mixture is smooth and well blended. Stir in the flour mixture until blended.

3. Scrape the dough onto a piece of plastic wrap and, using the wrap as a guide, shape it into a 2½-inch log. Wrap tightly and refrigerate for 3–4 hours, or freeze until hard.

4. Preheat the oven to 350°F. Line 2 large baking sheets with nonstick cookie parchment. Unwrap the dough and, using a sharp knife, cut the log into ¼-inch slices and place 1 inch apart on the baking sheets.

5. Bake for about 12 minutes, until lightly browned, rotating the baking sheets from the top to the bottom shelf and from front to back halfway through the cooking time. Remove the baking sheets to wire racks to cool for about 1 minute. Using a metal pancake turner, transfer each cookie to wire racks to cool completely.

6. Put the chocolate in a bowl over a pan of just simmering water. Stir until melted. Set aside to cool, stirring occasionally. When it reaches a spreading consistency, use a small spoon to swirl a little chocolate on each cookie. Sprinkle with a little candied ginger and allow the cookies to set. Store in airtight containers with waxed paper between the layers.

Coconut Lime Squares

Makes about 3 dozen

THESE COOKIES HAVE A DISTINCTLY COCONUT FLAVOR. IF YOU LIKE, ADD A FEW DROPS OF RUM EXTRACT INSTEAD OF ALMOND FOR A MORE CARIBBEAN FLAVOR.

2 cups plus 2 tablespoons all-purpose flour

½ teaspoon salt

1 cup (2 sticks) unsalted butter, softened

1 cup sugar

2 eggs, lightly beaten

Grated zest of 1 lime

½ teaspoon vanilla extract

½ teaspoon almond extract

1 tablespoon lime juice

¾ cup sweetened, shredded coconut, plus extra for decorating

Vegetable oil spray or vegetable oil, for greasing

1. Sift the flour and salt into a medium bowl. In a large bowl, beat the butter for 30 seconds, until creamy. Add the sugar and continue beating for 1–2 minutes, until light and fluffy. Beat in the eggs, lime zest, vanilla and almond extracts, and lime juice until well blended. Stir in the flour and shredded coconut.

2. Divide the dough in half and scrape onto two pieces of plastic wrap or waxed paper. Using the wrap or paper as a guide, form each dough half into a log about 2 inches in diameter. Flatten slightly on all sides to make a "square" log shape. Wrap tightly and refrigerate for several hours or overnight, until firm. The cookie dough can be made up to 5 days ahead, or frozen.

3. Preheat the oven to 375°F. Lightly spray or grease 2 large baking sheets. Unwrap and, using a sharp knife, cut the dough log into ¼-inch slices. Place the slices 1 inch apart on the baking sheets. Sprinkle each cookie with a little shredded coconut. Bake for about 10 minutes, until just golden. Remove the baking sheets to wire racks, then use a pancake turner to transfer the cookies onto wire racks to cool completely. Repeat with the remaining dough slices. Store in airtight containers.

Simple yet dynamic packaging for "Sunlight Creamery Butter," from the Cudahy Packing Company, dating around the 1930s decade.

Raspberry Jam Sandwiches

Makes about 18 cookies

GROUND ALMONDS MAKE AN ESPECIALLY FINE-TEXTURED COOKIE DOUGH. THESE TENDER COOKIE SQUARES CAN BE FILLED WITH ANY FLAVORED JAM THAT YOUR FAMILY AND FRIENDS PREFER.

1¼ cups blanched almonds

1½ cups all-purpose flour

¾ cup (1½ sticks) salted butter, softened

½ cup superfine sugar

1 egg, separated

Grated zest of 1 lemon

1 teaspoon vanilla extract

½ teaspoon salt

½ cup slivered almonds

1 cup raspberry jam

1 tablespoon lemon juice

1. Put the blanched almonds and ¼ cup of the flour in the bowl of a food processor. Using the metal blade, process until very finely ground.

2. In a large bowl, using an electric mixer, beat the butter for about 30 seconds, until creamy. Add the sugar and continue beating for 1–2 minutes, until light and fluffy. Beat in the egg yolk, lemon zest, and vanilla extract until well blended. On low speed, beat in the almond mixture, the remaining flour, and salt until well blended.

3. Scrape the dough onto a sheet of waxed paper or cling film and, using the paper or film as a guide, form into a flat disc. Refrigerate for 2 hours or overnight, until firm enough to handle. The dough can be made up to 2 days ahead.

4. Preheat the oven to 350°F. Line 2 baking sheets with nonstick baking parchment. On a lightly floured surface, using a floured rolling pin, roll half the dough into a square about 12 x 12 inches. Keep the remaining dough refrigerated. Cut the square crosswise into 6 strips, then lengthwise into 6 strips to make 24 2-inch squares. Using a floured ¾-inch round cutter, cut out the centers from half the rectangles. Alternatively, use a square fluted cutter and cut out as many squares from the dough as possible.

5. Using a pancake turner, transfer the squares to the baking sheets ½ inch apart. In a small bowl, whisk the egg white until frothy. Brush the top of the cookie rings only, then sprinkle each ring with a few slivered almonds. Bake for 8–10 minutes, until just golden. Remove the baking sheets to a wire rack to cool slightly, then transfer the cookies to wire racks to cool completely. Repeat with the remaining dough and trimmings.

6. In a small saucepan over low heat, heat the jam and lemon juice until melted. Spoon over the squares, then top with a cookie ring, pressing gently. Allow to set, then store in airtight containers with waxed paper between the layers.

Poppy Seed Spirals

Makes about 4 dozen cookies

POPPY SEED PASTE IS A POPULAR FILLING IN MANY GERMAN AND AUSTRIAN COFFEE CAKES. HERE IT IS USED IN THESE DELICIOUSLY CRISP COOKIE SPIRALS.

½ cup walnut pieces, finely ground

½ cup poppy seeds

⅓ cup honey

½ teaspoon ground cinnamon

Grated zest of 1 orange

6 tablespoons unsalted butter, softened

½ cup superfine sugar

1 egg, lightly beaten

1 teaspoon vanilla or rum extract

1½ cups all-purpose flour

Vegetable oil spray or vegetable oil, for greasing

1. In a small bowl, combine the ground walnuts, poppy seeds, honey, cinnamon, orange zest, and 2 tablespoons of softened butter, until the mixture forms a paste. Set aside.

2. In a large bowl, using an electric mixer, beat the remaining butter and sugar for 1–2 minutes, until light and fluffy. Beat in the egg and vanilla or rum extract until well blended, then slowly stir in the flour until a soft dough forms. Refrigerate the dough for 15–20 minutes, until firm enough to handle.

3. On a lightly floured sheet of waxed paper or nonstick baking parchment, roll out the dough to a rectangle about ¼-inch thick and spread with the poppy seed paste. Starting at one short side, roll up the dough jelly-roll fashion and wrap tightly in plastic wrap or foil. Refrigerate for several hours or overnight, until firm. The dough can be refrigerated for up to 5 days or frozen.

4. Preheat the oven to 375°F. Lightly spray or grease 2 large, nonstick baking sheets. Unwrap and slice the dough roll crosswise into ¼-inch slices and place ½ inch apart on the baking sheets. Bake for about 10 minutes, until golden; do not overbake. Remove the baking sheets to wire racks. Using a pancake turner, transfer the cookies to wire racks to cool. Repeat with the remaining slices. Store in airtight containers.

Hazelnut Marmalade Swirls

Makes about 4 dozen

These two-tone refrigerator cookies combine an orange-scented dough with a delicious marmalade chocolate-hazelnut filling.

1 cup hazelnuts, toasted and finely ground

½ cup orange marmalade

2 ounces semisweet chocolate, grated

½ teaspoon ground cinnamon

¼ teaspoon grated nutmeg

Zest of 1 grated orange

1 cup plus 3 tablespoons packed light brown sugar

¼ cup (½ stick) butter or margarine

¼ cup white vegetable shortening

1¾ cups all-purpose flour

1 egg

Vegetable oil spray or vegetable oil, for greasing

4 ounces semisweet chocolate, melted

1. In a bowl, combine the ground hazelnuts, orange marmalade, grated chocolate, cinnamon, nutmeg, 1 tablespoon of the orange zest, and 3 tablespoons of the sugar, until a spreadable paste forms.

2. In a medium bowl, using an electric mixer, beat the butter or margarine, shortening, flour, egg, remaining sugar, and orange zest until a stiff dough forms. Divide the dough in half.

3. On a piece of plastic wrap or waxed paper, roll out one piece of dough to a rectangle ¼-inch thick and spread with half the nut mixture. Starting at one short side, roll up the dough jelly-roll fashion and wrap tightly. Repeat with remaining dough and nut mixture. Refrigerate for several hours or overnight. The dough can be refrigerated up to 5 days or frozen.

4. Preheat the oven to 350°F. Lightly spray or grease 2 large baking sheets. Unwrap and slice one dough roll crosswise into ¼-inch slices and place 1 inch apart on the baking sheets. Bake for about 10 minutes,

This Umbrella Kids cookie jar was made by American Bisque, producers from 1930 to 1973.

until golden. Remove from the baking sheets to wire racks. Using a pancake turner, transfer the cookies to wire racks to cool. Repeat with remaining dough roll. Drizzle each cookie with a little melted chocolate and allow to set.

Variation

For a lemon-walnut cookie, use lemon marmalade, the zest of 1 grated lemon and walnuts instead of hazelnuts.

Spicy Gingerbread Cactus

Makes about 2 dozen cookies

GINGERBREAD COOKIES PROBABLY ORIGINATED IN GERMANY OR AUSTRIA, WHERE ELABORATE HOUSES WERE CONSTRUCTED FROM HARD-TEXTURED GINGERBREAD.

3½ cups all-purpose flour
1 teaspoon salt
1 teaspoon baking powder
1½ teaspoons ground ginger
1½ teaspoons ground cinnamon
1½ teaspoons allspice
1 teaspoon ground cloves
½ teaspoon cayenne pepper, or to taste
1 cup (2 sticks) unsalted butter or margarine, softened

⅔ cup packed dark brown sugar
½ cup light molasses
1 egg, lightly beaten
Vegetable oil spray or vegetable oil, for greasing

ROYAL ICING
2½ cups confectioner's sugar
¼ teaspoon cream tartar
2 egg whites
Food coloring (optional)
1 tablespoon lemon juice or rum

1. Sift the flour, salt, baking powder, ginger, cinnamon, allspice, cloves, and cayenne pepper into a medium bowl and set aside.

2. In another bowl, using an electric mixer, beat the butter or margarine and brown sugar for 1–2 minutes, until light and fluffy. Beat in the molasses and egg until blended. On low speed, beat in the flour mixture, until a soft dough forms.

3. Scrape the dough onto a piece of plastic wrap or cling film and, using the wrap or paper, shape into a flat disc. Wrap tightly and refrigerate for several hours or overnight, until firm enough to roll. The dough can be made up to 2 days ahead.

4. Preheat the oven to 350°F. Lightly spray or grease 2 large baking sheets. On a lightly floured surface, using a floured rolling pin, roll half the dough ¼-inch thick. Keep the remaining dough refrigerated. Using a floured cutter, cut out as many cookies as possible. Arrange 1 inch apart on the baking sheets.

5. Bake for about 10 minutes, until the edges of the cookies are lightly browned. Remove the

Black Engine & The Cookie Special Caboose, one of the famous McCoy jars produced from 1961 to 1964.

baking sheets to wire racks. Using a pancake turner, transfer the cookies to wire racks to cool completely. Repeat with the remaining cookie dough and dough trimmings.

6. Sift the confectioner's sugar and cream of tartar into a medium bowl. Using an electric mixer, beat in the egg whites until well mixed, then increase the speed and continue beating until the whites are stiff and the beaters leave a clean path in the bottom of the bowl. If you like, divide the icing into small bowls and add a few drops of food coloring to each portion. Add a little lemon juice or rum to achieve a spreading consistency. Spoon icing or icings into one or more paper cones (see page 19), and pipe decorations onto the cookies. Allow to dry for 2 hours at room temperature. Store in airtight containers.

Moravian Spice Squares

Makes about 2½ dozen cookies

¼ cup (½ stick) unsalted butter

¼ cup packed dark brown sugar

2 tablespoons molasses

1¼ cups all-purpose flour

Grated zest of 1 lemon

1 teaspoon ground ginger

1 teaspoon ground cinnamon

¼ teaspoon ground cloves

½ teaspoon baking soda

Vegetable oil spray or vegetable oil, for greasing

Sugar, for sprinkling

1. In a medium saucepan over medium heat, heat the butter, brown sugar, and molasses until melted and smooth, stirring often. Remove from the heat and stir in the flour, lemon zest, ginger, cinnamon, cloves, and baking soda until blended.

2. Scrape the dough onto a piece of waxed paper or plastic wrap and, using the paper or wrap as a guide, shape into a flat disc. Wrap tightly and refrigerate for several hours or overnight. The dough can be made up to 5 days ahead.

3. Preheat the oven to 350°F. Lightly spray or grease 2 large baking sheets. On a lightly floured surface, using a floured rolling pin, roll one half of the dough into a 10 x 10-inch square. Using a sharp knife or pastry wheel, cut the dough into 1¼-inch squares and place about 1 inch apart on the baking sheet.

4. With a fork, gently prick the cookie squares to prevent the pastry puffing, and sprinkle with a little sugar. Bake for 7 minutes, until just set. Using a pancake turner, transfer to wire racks to cool completely. Repeat with the remaining dough. Store in airtight containers.

Shrewsbury Biscuits

Makes about 3 dozen

1 cup (2 sticks) unsalted butter

1 cup superfine sugar

1 egg, beaten

¼ cup heavy cream

1 tablespoon dry sherry

½ cup dried currants

1–1¼ cups all-purpose flour, sifted

Superfine sugar, for sprinkling

1. In a large bowl, using an electric mixer, beat the butter and sugar for 1–2 minutes, until light and creamy. Beat in the egg, cream, sherry, and currants. Stir in the flour until a soft dough forms.

2. Scrape out onto plastic wrap and, using the wrap as a guide, shape into a flat disc. Refrigerate for 1 hour, until firm.

3. Preheat the oven to 350°F. Grease 2 large baking sheets. On a lightly floured surface, roll out the dough ¼-inch thick. With a 2½-inch cutter, cut out rounds. Place 1 inch apart on baking sheets.

4. Brush with water, and sprinkle with a little superfine sugar. Bake for about 15 minutes, until crisp and just beginning to brown.

Chocolate Pistachio Pinwheels

Makes about 3 dozen cookies

2½ cups all-purpose flour

2 tablespoons unsweetened cocoa powder

2½ teaspoons baking powder

½ teaspoon salt

½ cup (1 stick) unsalted butter, softened

½ cup superfine sugar

1 egg, lightly beaten

2 tablespoons light corn syrup

Vegetable oil spray or vegetable oil, for greasing

1½ cups finely chopped pistachio or macadamia nuts

1. Sift the flour, cocoa powder, baking powder, and salt into a medium bowl.

2. In a large bowl, using an electric mixer, beat the butter and sugar for 1–2 minutes, until light and creamy. Beat in the egg and corn syrup until blended, then stir in the flour mixture. Turn the dough onto a lightly floured surface and knead lightly until smooth. Wrap tightly in plastic wrap or waxed paper and refrigerate for about ½ hour, until firm enough to roll.

3. Preheat the oven to 350°F. Lightly spray or grease 2 large baking sheets. On a lightly floured surface, using a floured rolling pin, roll out the dough ⅛ inch thick. Using a floured 3½-inch round or square cutter, cut out rounds or squares.

4. Place the cut-outs on the baking sheets. With a knife and beginning at the outside edge, make 4 cuts almost to the center forming quarters (if a square cutter has been used, make a diagonal cut from each corner). Fold the left corner of each corner to the center and press to seal, forming a pinwheel shape. Sprinkle the center with nuts.

5. Bake for about 10 minutes, until firm. Remove the sheets to wire racks to cool slightly. Transfer the cookies to wire racks to cool completely.

A variety of heart-shaped cookie cutters made in Germany—a set of 3 corrugated around the outside, and a 2-piece plain-edged set.

Christmas Cut-out Cookies

Makes about 6 dozen (depending on the size of the cutters)

AMERICAN CHRISTMAS COOKIES CAN BE TRACED BACK TO AUSTRO-GERMAN ROOTS. USE THIS LEMONY SUGAR COOKIE AS A BASE TO FORM LOTS OF CHRISTMAS SHAPES. LOOK OUT FOR INTERESTING COOKIE CUTTERS, FROM ANGELS TO REINDEERS.

2 cups all-purpose flour

2 teaspoon baking powder

½ teaspoon salt

½ cup (1 stick) unsalted butter, softened

1 cup superfine sugar

1 egg, lightly beaten

Grated zest of 1 lemon

1 tablespoon lemon juice

1 tablespoon vanilla extract

½ teaspoon lemon extract

ICING

3 cups confectioner's sugar

2–3 tablespoons milk

1 tablespoon lemon juice

Red and green food coloring (optional)

1. Sift the flour, baking powder, and salt into a medium bowl. In a large bowl, using an electric mixer, beat the butter for about 30 seconds, until creamy. Add the sugar and continue beating for 1–2 minutes, until light and fluffy. Beat in the egg, lemon zest and juice, and vanilla and lemon extracts until well blended. Stir in the flour mixture until well blended and a soft dough forms.

2. Form the dough into a ball and flatten to a disc shape. Wrap tightly and refrigerate for several hours or overnight, until the dough is firm enough to handle.

3. Preheat the oven to 350°F. On a lightly floured surface, using a floured rolling pin, roll out one third of the dough ⅛-inch thick. Keep the remaining dough refrigerated. Using floured cookie cutters, cut out as many shapes as possible and, if

necessary, use a thin-bladed metal spatula to transfer the shapes to 2 large, ungreased baking sheets, placing them 1 inch apart.

4. Bake for about 8 minutes, until the cookies are just colored around the edges. Using a pancake turner, transfer the cookies to wire racks to cool completely. Repeat rolling, cutting, and baking with the remaining dough.

5. Sift the confectioner's sugar into a medium bowl. Stir in 2 tablespoons of milk and lemon juice, adding a little more milk if the icing is too thick. Spoon about one-third of the icing into a small bowl and another third into another small bowl. Add a few drops of red coloring to one bowl and green to the other, mixing until you achieve the desired shades.

6. Spoon the 3 colors into 3 paper cones (see page 19). Pipe designs onto each shape. Allow to set for about 2 hours, then store in airtight containers with waxed paper between the layers.

This delightful Father Christmas cookie jar is a Limited Edition Saks Fifth Avneue item—much sought after by collectors.

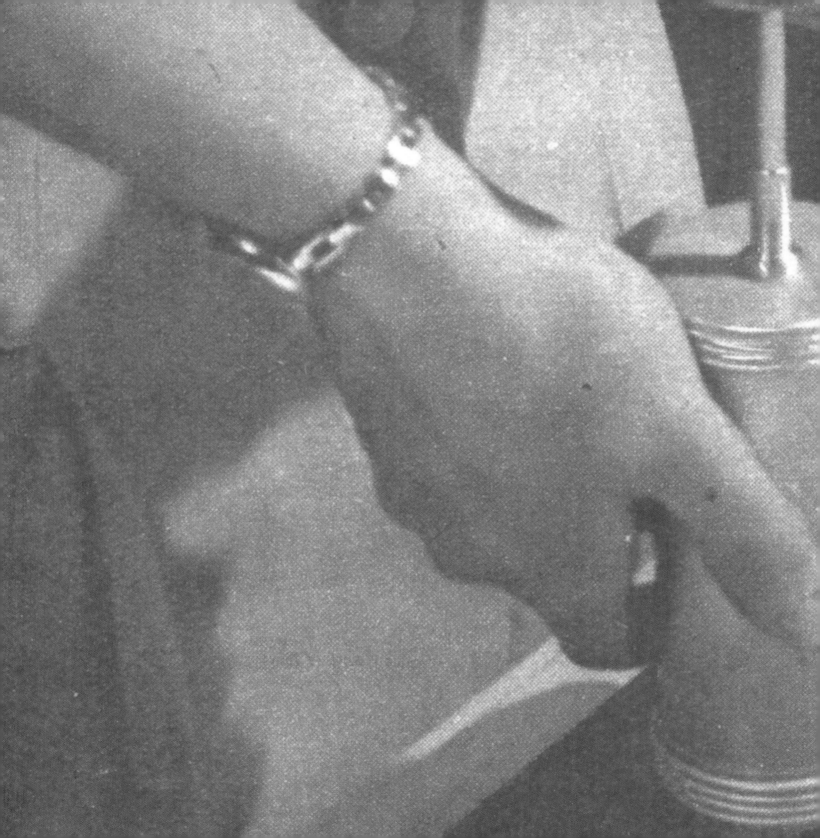

Pressed & Piped Cookies

Chocolate-Dipped Lime Ribbons

Makes about 30 cookies

To pipe cookies, they must be of a soft enough consistency. In this recipe, the egg white is folded into the dough to give it just the right texture.

Vegetable oil spray or vegetable oil, for greasing

¾ cup all-purpose flour

2 tablespoons cornstarch

⅛ teaspoon baking powder

½ cup (1 stick) unsalted butter, softened

⅓ cup confectioner's sugar

1 egg, separated

Grated zest of 1 large lime

1 tablespoon fresh lime juice

½ teaspoon vanilla extract

⅛ teaspoon salt

Sugar, for sprinkling

4 ounces semisweet chocolate, melted

1 ounce pistachio nuts, finely chopped

1. Preheat the oven to 350°F. Lightly spray or or grease 2 large baking sheets. Sift the flour, cornstarch, and baking powder into a medium bowl.

A trade card of 1895 featuring B. T. Babbitt's Baking Powder.

2. In a large bowl, using an electric mixer, beat the butter and sugar for 1–2 minutes, until light and fluffy. Beat in the egg yolk, lime zest, lime juice, and vanilla extract until well blended. Stir in the flour mixture until well blended and set aside.

3. In a small bowl, using an electric mixer with cleaned beaters, beat the egg white and salt until stiff peaks form. Gently fold into the dough until blended; the dough should be soft.

4. Spoon the dough into a pastry bag fitted with a medium ribbon tip. Pipe 2-inch lengths l inch apart onto the baking sheets and sprinkle each cookie with a little sugar.

5. Bake for about 10 minutes, until set and the edges are golden. Remove the baking sheets to wire racks to cool for 3–5 minutes. Using a pancake turner, transfer the cookies to wire racks.

6. Dip the end of each cookie into melted chocolate and place on a waxed paper-lined baking sheet, then sprinkle with a few chopped pistachios. Allow the chocolate to set. Store the cookies in airtight containers with waxed paper between the layers.

Chocolate Amaretti

Makes about 2 dozen cookies

Surprisingly easy to make, these chocolate-almond cookies resemble a rich, chewy macaroon. Be sure the dough is firm enough to pipe.

1 cup blanched whole almonds

½ cup superfine sugar

1 tablespoon unsweetened cocoa powder (preferably Dutch-processed)

2 tablespoons confectioner's sugar

2 medium egg whites

⅛ teaspoon cream of tartar

½ teaspoon vanilla extract

½ teaspoon almond extract

Slivered almonds, to decorate (optional)

1. Preheat the oven to 350°F. Spread the blanched almonds on a small baking sheet and toast for 7–10 minutes, until golden and fragrant. Pour onto a plate to cool completely. Reduce the oven temperature to 325°F. Line a large baking sheet with nonstick baking parchment or lightly greased foil.

2. Put the toasted almonds and 2 tablespoons of superfine sugar into the bowl of a food processor. Using the metal blade, process until finely ground but not oily. Add the cocoa powder and confectioner's sugar, and using the pulse action, process to blend well.

3. In a medium bowl, beat the egg whites until foamy. Add the cream of tartar and continue beating until stiff peaks form. Sprinkle in the remaining superfine sugar, a tablespoon at a time, beating well after each addition, until the whites are stiff and glossy. Beat in the vanilla and almond extracts, then gently fold in the almond-cocoa mixture until just blended.

4. Spoon the mixture into a large pastry bag fitted with a medium plain ½-inch tip. Pipe 1½-inch mounds 1 inch apart onto the baking sheet. If you like, sprinkle a few slivered almonds onto the center of each mound.

5. Bake for 10–12 minutes, until the cookies are firm on top when touched with a fingertip and the surface is slightly crisp. Remove the baking sheet to a wire rack to cool slightly. Using a pancake turner, remove the cookies to a wire rack to cool completely. Store in an airtight container.

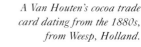

A Van Houten's cocoa trade card dating from the 1880s, from Weesp, Holland.

Spiral Spice Cookies

Makes about 1 dozen cookies

Spice-cookie doughs were popular in New England and the Pennsylvania Dutch Country, especially in the autumn. Look out for whole nutmegs.

1½ cups all-purpose flour

½ teaspoon baking soda

1 teaspoon ground cinnamon

½ teaspoon freshly grated nutmeg

½ teaspoon ground ginger

½ teaspoon ground cardamom

¼ teaspoon finely ground black pepper

⅛ teaspoon salt

⅓ cup white vegetable shortening

⅓ sugar

⅓ cup molasses

1 egg

2 tablespoons cider vinegar

Vegetable oil spray or vegetable oil, for greasing

Confectioner's sugar, for dusting

1. Sift the flour, baking soda, cinnamon, nutmeg, ginger, cardamom, black pepper, and salt into a medium bowl.

2. In a large bowl, using an electric mixer, beat the shortening and sugar for 1–2 minutes, until light and fluffy. Beat in the molasses, egg, and vinegar until blended. On low speed, beat in the flour-spice mixture until a soft dough forms.

3. Preheat the oven to 350°F. Lightly spray or grease 2 large baking sheets. Spoon the dough into a large pastry bag fitted with a ¼-inch plain tip. Pipe the dough into 3-inch circles, beginning at the center point and working to the outer edge, 2 inches apart on the baking sheets.

4. Bake for about 10 minutes, until just set and beginning to brown at the edge. Remove the baking sheets to wire racks. Using a pancake turner, transfer the cookies to wire racks to cool completely. Lightly dust with confectioner's sugar. Store in airtight containers.

Chocolate Viennese Fingers

Makes about 2 dozen cookies

THIS BUTTER-RICH AUSTRIAN COOKIE IS FOUND IN THE KONDITERI OF VIENNA. ITS FLAVOR AS WELL AS ITS SHAPE IS ACCENTUATED BY DIPPING INTO MELTED CHOCOLATE.

Vegetable oil spray or vegetable oil, for greasing

2 cups all purpose flour

⅓ cup unsweetened cocoa powder (preferably Dutch-processed)

¼ cup cornstarch

1 cup (2 sticks) unsalted butter, softened

½ cup confectioner's sugar, sifted

1 teaspoon vanilla extract

Confectioner's sugar, for dusting

4 ounces bittersweet or semisweet chocolate, melted (optional)

1. Preheat the oven to 350°F. Lightly spray or grease 2 large baking sheets. Sift the flour, cocoa powder, and cornstarch into a medium bowl.

2. In a large bowl, using an electric mixer, beat the butter and confectioner's sugar for 1–2 minutes, until light and fluffy. On low speed, gradually beat in the flour

mixture and vanilla extract until a soft dough forms.

3. Spoon the dough into a large pastry bag fitted with a large star tip. Pipe about 24 3-inch fingers or "S" shapes 2 inches apart on the baking sheets.

4. Bake for 15–20 minutes, until set and slightly firm when touched with a fingertip, rotating the baking sheets from the top to the bottom shelf and from front to back halfway through the cooking

This Polka Dot Witch is an outstanding example of the "new American classic" cookie jars.

time. Remove the baking sheets to wire racks to cool for about 15 minutes, until the cookies are firm. Using a pancake turner, transfer the cookies to wire racks to cool completely.

5. Arrange close together on a wire rack and dust with confectioner's sugar. Drizzle with melted chocolate, or dip one end of each cookie halfway into the chocolate and tap off any excess. Place on a wax paper-lined baking sheet and allow to set. Store in airtight containers with waxed paper between the layers.

Spritz Cookies

Makes about 4½ dozen cookies

Spritz cookies are a tender, rich butter cookie made with a cookie press. A variety of design plates produce several different shapes, but the dough must be just the right consistency.

1 cup (2 sticks) unsalted butter, softened

½ cup superfine sugar

1 egg, lightly beaten

1½ teaspoons vanilla or 1 teaspoon almond extract

2–2½ cups all-purpose flour, sifted

Sugar sprinkles or other cookie decorations, to decorate

1. Preheat the oven to 375°F. In a large bowl, using an electric mixer, beat the butter for 30–60 seconds, until creamy. Add the sugar and continue beating for 1–2 minutes, until the mixture is light and fluffy. Beat in the egg and vanilla or almond extract. On low speed, gradually beat in 2¼ cups flour until a soft dough forms. Add a little more flour if the dough is too soft.*

2. Pack the cookie dough into a cookie press fitted with the design plate of your choice. Press out cookies onto 2 cold, ungreased baking sheets. Depending on the shape, sprinkle each cookie with a few sprinkles, or other cookie decorations, or press a candied cherry into the center of each cookie. Bake for about 8 minutes, until set and just golden. Remove the baking sheets to wire racks to cool slightly. Using a thin-bladed metal spatula, transfer the cookies to wire racks to cool completely. Clean and chill the baking sheets and repeat with the remaining cookie dough. Store the cookies in airtight containers.

* Cookie press cookies can be difficult to form unless the dough is the right temperature. If the dough or weather is too warm, the dough won't hold its shape and may have to be chilled for about ½ hour before pressing. If the dough is chilled too long or is too firm, it will be difficult to press through the design plate.

To stiffen the dough, add a little more flour. If too stiff, add a little milk. Form a log shape slightly smaller than the diameter of the cookie press and insert into the prepared press. Every cookie press has its own directions, which you should read thoroughly. You may want to practice with a few turns.

Strawberry Thumbprints

Makes about 4½ dozen cookies

Pressing a thumb into each cookie mound gives these classic cookies their name. For a fancier cookie, the dough can be piped with a star tip.

¾ cup (1½ sticks) unsalted butter, softened

½ cup sugar

2 eggs, lightly beaten

1 teaspoon vanilla extract

½ teaspoon ground cinnamon

¼ teaspoon salt

2 cups all-purpose flour

⅔ cup strawberry preserves or other favorite jam or jelly

1. Preheat the oven to 400°F. In a large bowl, using an electric mixer, beat the butter for 30 seconds, until creamy. Add the sugar and beat for 1–2 minutes, until light and fluffy. Gradually beat in the eggs, vanilla extract, cinnamon, and salt. Stir in the flour until a soft dough forms.

2. Spoon the dough into a large pastry bag fitted with a plain ½-inch tip. Pipe 1½-inch rounds 1 inch apart on 2 large, ungreased baking sheets. Press a lightly floured thumb into the center of each round, making a deep depression.

3. Bake the cookies for about 8 minutes, until golden. If the hole fills in, use the end of a wooden spoon handle to accentuate the indentations. Remove the baking sheets to wire racks. Using a pancake turner, transfer the cookies to wire racks to cool.

4. While the cookies are still warm, heat the strawberry preserves in a small saucepan over low heat, until just beginning to bubble. Using a small teaspoon, spoon a little of the preserves into each indentation. Allow the cookies and jam to set and cool completely. Store the cookies in airtight containers in single layers.

A color illustration of Standard Sugar Cookies from a pamphlet produced by the John F Jelke Company in 1927, featuring their "Good Luck" margarine.

Almond-Meringue Cream Sandwiches

Makes about 14 sandwiches or 28 meringues

CLASSIC MERINGUES SANDWICHED WITH WHIPPED CREAM ARE ONE OF THE FAVORITE FANCY COOKIES PRESENTED AT A SPECIAL TEATIME.

4 egg whites

⅛ teaspoon cream of tartar

1¼ cups superfine sugar

½ teaspoon almond extract

1 cup blanched almonds, toasted and coarsely chopped

1 cup heavy or whipping cream

1–2 tablespoons Amaretto liqueur, to serve

1. Preheat the oven to 200°F. Line 2 large baking sheets with foil or nonstick baking parchment.

2. In a large bowl, using an electric mixer, beat the egg whites until foamy. Add the cream of tartar and continue beating on high speed until stiff peaks form. Gradually add the sugar a tablespoon at a time, beating well after each addition, until the whites are stiff and glossy. Beat in the almond extract and gently fold in the chopped almonds.

3. Gently spoon the mixture into a large pastry bag fitted with a large star tip. Pipe an even number of 1½–2 inch rosettes 1½ inches apart on the prepared baking sheets.

4. Bake the meringues for about 1 hour, until set and cooked through, rotating the baking sheets from the top to the bottom shelf and front to back halfway through the cooking time. Do not allow the

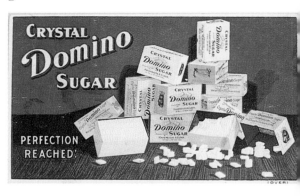

A trade card originating from New York city, dating back to the 1880s and 1890s.

meringues to brown at all. Turn off the oven but do not remove the meringues; allow them to stay in the oven for a further 1 hour. Remove the baking sheets from the oven and peel the meringues off the foil or paper. Arrange on wire racks to cool completely. Store unfilled meringues in airtight containers.

5. To serve, whip the cream and Amaretto in a medium bowl until stiff peaks form. Spread a little cream on one meringue and sandwich with another. Continue with the remaining meringues and cream.

This Howdy Doody Vandor cookie jar is not only a "character jar" but also a "head jar"—a category in which some collectors specialize.

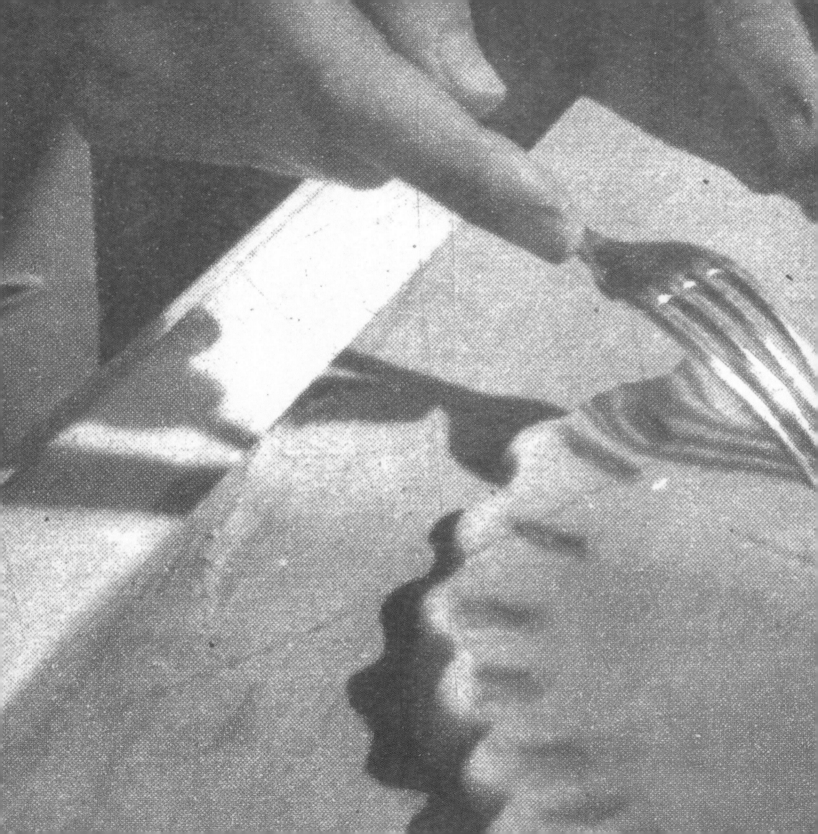

Bar Cookies

Chocolate-Pecan Brownies

Makes about 2 dozen squares

Brownies must be dense and fudgy; adding extra chocolate, pecans, and a dark buttery chocolate glaze makes them extra special.

Vegetable oil spray or vegetable oil, for greasing

4 ounces unsweetened chocolate, chopped

¾ cup (1½ sticks) butter, cut into pieces

1¾ cups sugar

3 eggs

1 teaspoon vanilla extract

1½ cups pecans

1 cup semisweet chocolate chips (optional)

1 cup all-purpose flour

CHOCOLATE GLAZE

6 ounces bittersweet or semisweet chocolate, chopped

½ cup heavy cream

2 tablespoons unsalted butter, cut into pieces

1 teaspoon vanilla extract

24 perfect pecan halves, to decorate (optional)

1. Preheat the oven to 350°F. Invert a 13 x 9-inch baking pan. Mold a sheet of foil over the bottom of the pan, smoothing it evenly around the corners. Remove the foil and turn the pan right side up. Press the foil into the pan, smoothing it into the sides and corners. Lightly spray or grease.

2. Melt the chocolate and butter in a medium saucepan over low heat, until melted and smooth, stirring frequently.

Remove from the heat and stir in the sugar until blended. Beat in the eggs, one at a time, beating well after each addition. Stir in the vanilla extract, nuts, and chocolate chips. Stir in the flour until just blended—the batter will be stiff. Spread in the pan, smoothing the top evenly.

3. Bake for about 25 minutes, until a cake tester or toothpick inverted in the center comes out with sticky crumbs attached. Be very careful not to overbake the brownies. Remove from the pan to a wire rack to cool completely.

4. Melt the chocolate and cream in a medium saucepan over low heat, until melted and smooth, stirring frequently. Remove from the heat to cool slightly. Whisk in the butter and vanilla. Cool the remaining glaze until thickened and spreadable.

5. Using the foil as a guide, remove the brownies from the pan and invert onto a board. Using a thin-bladed metal spatula, spread the brownies with

the glaze. Refrigerate for at least 1 hour, until set. Using a long-bladed sharp knife, cut the brownies into 24 squares. Press a pecan half into the center of each brownie square, if used. Store in airtight containers in single layers.

Variation

For easy unglazed brownies, refrigerate for 1 hour before cutting into squares. Dust squares with confectioner's sugar.

Chocolate Raspberry Macaroon Bars

Makes about 2 dozen bars

CHOCOLATE COOKIE CRUST

Vegetable oil spray or vegetable oil, for greasing

½ cup (1 stick) unsalted butter, softened

½ cup confectioner's sugar, sifted

¼ cup unsweetened cocoa powder (preferably Dutch-processed), sifted

¼ teaspoon salt

1 teaspoon vanilla or almond extract

1 cup all-purpose flour

TOPPING

½ cup seedless raspberry preserves

1 tablespoon raspberry flavor liqueur (optional)

1 cup mini semisweet, or milk chocolate chips

1½ cups finely ground blanched almonds

4 egg whites

¼ teaspoon salt

1 cup superfine sugar

½ teaspoon almond extract

¼ cup slivered almonds

Confectioner's sugar, for dusting (optional)

A DARK CHOCOLATE CRUST TOPPED WITH RASPBERRY PRESERVES AND AN ALMOND TOPPING BAKES TO A CHEWY TEXTURE.

1. Preheat the oven to 325°F. Invert a 13 x 9-inch baking pan. Mold foil over the bottom of the pan, smoothing it evenly around the corners. Remove the foil and turn the pan right side up. Press the foil into the pan, smoothing it into the sides and corners. Spray or grease the foil.

2. In a medium bowl, using an electric mixer, beat the butter, confectioner's sugar, cocoa powder, and salt for 1–2 minutes, until creamy. Beat in the vanilla or almond extract. On low speed, beat in the flour until a crumbly dough forms.

3. Turn the dough into the pan and pat firmly over the bottom to create a thin, even layer. Prick the dough with a fork. Bake for about 20 minutes, until set. Remove from the oven to a wire rack and increase the oven temperature to 375°F.

4. Combine the raspberry preserves and liqueur in a small bowl. Spread evenly

A chopping knife with a crescent blade, dating from the end of the 19th century.

over the crust, then sprinkle with the chocolate chips.

5. Put the ground almonds, egg whites, salt, superfine sugar, and almond extract in a food processor. Using the metal blade, process the ingredients. Gently pour over the jam and chocolate chip layer, spreading evenly to the sides of the pan. Sprinkle with the slivered almonds.

6. Bake for about 25 minutes, until the top is lightly browned and puffed. Remove to a wire rack and cool for about half an hour, until firm enough to handle. Using the foil as a guide, remove from the pan and cool on a wire rack. When cold, peel off the foil and place on a board. Cut into bars and dust with confectioner's sugar, if you like. Store in airtight containers in single layers.

Lemon Bars

Makes about 30 bars

A Touch of Sweetness with the Flavor of Lemon

Lemon Snaps 5¢
NATIONAL BISCUIT COMPANY

LEMON BARS ARE ONE OF MY FAVORITE COOKIES, PROBABLY BECAUSE THEY REMIND ME OF THE CLASSIC FRENCH *TARTE AU CITRON*.

SHORTBREAD CRUST

Vegetable oil spray or vegetable oil, for greasing

1½ cups all-purpose flour

½ cup confectioner's sugar

½ teaspoon salt

¾ cup (1½ sticks) cold unsalted butter, cut into small pieces

1 teaspoon grated lemon zest

LEMON TOPPING

4 eggs

1½ cups superfine sugar

Grated zest of 1 lemon

½ cup fresh lemon juice

¾ cup heavy cream

Confectioner's sugar, for dusting

1. Preheat the oven to 325°F. Invert a 13 x 9-inch baking pan. Mold foil over the bottom of the pan, smoothing it evenly around the corners. Remove the foil and turn the pan right side up. Press the foil into the pan, smoothing it into the sides and corners. Spray or grease the foil.

2. Sift the flour, sugar, and salt into a large bowl. Sprinkle over the butter and lemon zest. Using a pastry blender or fingertips, cut in the butter until coarse crumbs form and the dough begins to stick together.

3. Turn into the pan and pat firmly over the bottom to form an even layer, smoothing the surface. Bake for about 20 minutes, until just golden. Remove the pan to a wire rack to cool slightly.

4. In a medium bowl, beat the eggs and sugar for 3–5 minutes, until fluffy. Beat in the lemon zest and juice.

5. In another bowl, using cleaned beaters, beat the cream until soft peaks form. Fold into the egg mixture in 2 batches and pour over the base. Return the pan to the oven and bake for about 40 minutes, until the topping is set. Remove the pan to a wire rack to cool.

6. Using the foil as a guide, remove from the pan and set on a board. Peel off the foil and cut into bars. Dust lightly with confectioner's sugar.

Date-Filled Oat Crumb Squares

Makes about 2 dozen squares

This delicious bar cookie is a mixture of an oaty base and crumbly topping with a rich date purée filling.

FILLING
1 pound pitted dates
1 cup packed light brown sugar
1 cup water
1 teaspoon vanilla extract
½ teaspoon ground cinnamon

CRUST
Vegetable oil spray or vegetable oil, for greasing
1½ cups old-fashioned oats
1½ cups all-purpose flour
1 cup packed light brown sugar
1 teaspoon ground cinnamon
½ teaspoon baking soda
½ cup chopped walnuts or pecans
1 cup (2 sticks) cold unsalted butter, cut into small pieces

1. Simmer the dates, sugar, and water in a medium saucepan over medium heat, until the sugar dissolves and all the liquid is evaporated. Remove from the heat and stir in the vanilla extract and cinnamon. Pour into a food processor and, using the metal blade, process the mixture until just smooth. Pour into a bowl to cool.

2. Invert a 13 x 9-inch baking pan. Mold foil over the bottom, smoothing it evenly around the corners. Remove the foil and turn the pan right side up. Press the foil into the pan, smoothing into the sides and corners. Spray or grease.

3. Preheat the oven to 350°F. In a large bowl, combine the oats, flour, brown sugar, cinnamon, baking soda, and walnuts or pecans. Sprinkle over the cut-up butter and, using a pastry blender or your fingertips, cut in the butter until coarse crumbs form.

4. Turn half the mixture into the pan and pat firmly into the bottom and sides to form a lower crust, smoothing the surface. Spread the filling over the crust, then evenly sprinkle over the remaining crumb mixture.

5. Bake for about 35 minutes, until the topping is browned and the filling is sizzling. Remove the pan to a wire rack to cool for about 1 hour. Using the foil as a guide, remove from the pan and set on a board. Peel off the foil and cut into squares or bars.

Variation
Use 1 pound of dried apricots in place of the pitted dates.

Chewy Caramel Nut Squares

Makes about 3 dozen squares

THIS CHEWY BAR COOKIE IS A NUT LOVER'S DREAM. A RICH, HONEY-FLAVORED CARAMEL TOPPING, FILLED WITH A COMBINATION OF NUTS, COVERS A RICH PASTRY.

PASTRY CRUST

Vegetable oil spray or vegetable oil, for greasing

3 cups all-purpose flour

½ cup cornstarch

½ teaspoon salt

1½ cups (3 sticks) unsalted butter, softened

⅔ cup sugar

Grated zest of 1 lemon

CARAMEL NUT TOPPING

10 tablespoons (1¼ sticks) unsalted butter

½ cup packed dark brown sugar

½ cup honey

1½ tablespoons whipping cream

1 cup salted cashews, lightly toasted and coarsely chopped

1 cup whole blanched almonds, toasted and coarsely chopped

1 cup pine nuts, toasted

1. Invert a 13 x 9-inch baking pan. Mold foil over the bottom, smoothing it evenly around the corners. Remove the foil and turn the pan right side up. Press the foil into the pan, smoothing it into the sides and corners. Spray or grease the foil.

2. Preheat the oven to 350°F. Sift the flour, cornstarch, and salt into a medium bowl. In a large bowl, using an electric mixer, beat the butter, sugar, and lemon zest for 1–2 minutes, until light and fluffy. On low speed, beat in the flour mixture, until blended and a soft dough forms.

3. Press the dough evenly onto the bottom and 1 inch up the sides of the pan, pressing into the corners. Prick the bottom with a fork and bake for about 30 minutes, until the pastry is very lightly browned, turning the pan halfway through cooking and pricking with a fork if the pastry puffs up. Remove the pan to a wire rack.

4. In a medium saucepan over medium heat, bring to a boil the

This Winnie the Pooh "Hunny Pot" jar is an old favorite, produced by California Originals.

butter, sugar, honey, and cream, stirring until the sugar dissolves. Boil, without stirring, for about 1 minute, until the mixture thickens slightly. Remove from the heat and stir in the cashews, almonds, and pine nuts until well mixed.

5. Pour the nut mixture over the crust, spreading evenly. Bake for about 20 minutes, until sticky and bubbling. Remove to a wire rack to cool completely. Using the foil as a guide, remove to a board. Peel off the foil and cut into 1½-inch squares. Store in airtight containers in single layers.

Butterscotch Bars with Meringue Topping

Makes about 1 dozen bars

BUTTERSCOTCH COOKIE LAYER

Vegetable oil spray or vegetable oil, for greasing

¼ cup (½ stick) unsalted butter

1 cup packed dark brown sugar

½ cup all-purpose flour

1 teaspoon ground cinnamon

½ teaspoon salt

1 egg

1 teaspoon vanilla extract

MERINGUE TOPPING

1 egg white

⅛ teaspoon cream of tartar

1 tablespoon corn syrup

½ cup superfine sugar

1 cup chopped walnuts

A WALNUT-ENRICHED, CRACKLY MERINGUE TOPPING COVERS AN EASY BUTTERSCOTCH COOKIE LAYER—SWEET BUT IRRESISTIBLE!

1. Preheat the oven to 350°F. Invert an 8-inch square baking pan. Mold a sheet of foil over the bottom of the pan, smoothing it evenly around the corners. Remove the foil and turn the pan right side up. Press the foil into the pan, smoothing it into the sides and corners. Spray or grease the foil.

2. In a medium saucepan over medium heat, simmer the butter and brown sugar for about 3–5 minutes, until the sugar dissolves. Remove from the heat and cool. Sift the flour, cinnamon, and salt into a medium bowl.

3. Beat the egg and vanilla extract into the cooled butter mixture until well blended. Stir in the flour mixture until just blended. Spread over the bottom of the pan, smoothing the surface evenly.

4. In a medium bowl, beat the egg white until foamy. Add the cream of tartar and continue beating until soft peaks form. Gradually beat in the corn syrup, then the sugar and continue beating until the whites are stiff and glossy. Fold in half the nuts and carefully spread the topping over the butterscotch layer. Sprinkle the top with the remaining nuts.

5. Bake for about 30 minutes, until the topping is puffed (the meringue may crack) and golden. Remove to a wire rack and cool completely. Using the foil as a guide, remove to a board and peel off the foil. Cut into 1½-inch fingers. Store in airtight containers in single layers.

Scottish Shortbread

Makes 16 large wedges or 32 thin wedges

THIS FAMOUS SCOTTISH COOKIE IS SIMPLE BUT SO GOOD. BECAUSE THERE ARE SO FEW INGREDIENTS, THEY MUST BE FIRST CLASS. BUY THE BEST, FRESHEST SWEET BUTTER.

Vegetable spray oil or butter, for greasing

¼ cup confectioner's sugar

¼ cup superfine sugar

¼ teaspoon salt

10 tablespoons (1¼ sticks) unsalted butter, softened

1½ cups all-purpose flour

1. Preheat the oven to 275°F. Lightly spray or brush with softened butter two 8-inch tart or cake pans with removable bottoms. Sift the confectioner's sugar into a large bowl. Add the superfine sugar and salt, and mix well. Add the butter and, using an electric mixer, beat the butter and sugars for 1–2 minutes, until light and fluffy. Stir in the flour in 2–3 batches until well blended. On a lightly floured surface, knead the dough very lightly to ensure an even blending.

2. Divide the dough evenly between the pans and pat onto the bottoms in even layers. Using a kitchen fork, press ¾-inch radiating lines around the edge of the dough. Prick the surface lightly with a fork (this helps keep an even surface as well as creating the traditional pattern). If you like, score each shortbread dough round into 8 or 16 wedges for easier cutting later.

3. Bake for about 40 minutes, until pale golden (do not brown—shortbread should be very pale), rotating the pans halfway through cooking. Reduce the oven temperature if the shortbread begins to color too quickly. Remove the pans to a wire rack to cool for 10 minutes.

A 24-pound bag of "Gaebe's Best Flour," from J. H. Gaebe & Co. of Addieville, Illinois.

The Educated Tree—a rare cookie jar produced by the Metlox company of Manhattan Beach, California. Metlox began making jars in 1947.

4. Carefully remove the side of each pan and place the pan bottoms onto a heatproof surface. Cut each shortbread circle into 8 wide or 16 thin wedges, following the scored marks, if used. This must be done while the shortbread is warm and soft, or it will break. Return the shortbread wedges on their bases to wire racks to cool completely.

Special Cookies

French Almond Tile Cookies

Makes about 2½ dozen

THESE POPULAR FRENCH COOKIES—*TUILES AUX AMANDES*—ARE SO-CALLED BECAUSE THEY RESEMBLE THE CURVED ROOF TILES SEEN ALL OVER FRANCE.

½ cup whole blanched almonds, lightly toasted

½ cup superfine sugar

Butter, for greasing

3 tablespoons unsalted butter, softened

2 egg whites

½ teaspoon almond extract

¼ cup cake flour, sifted

¼ cup flaked almonds

1. Put the blanched almonds and 2 tablespoons of the sugar in the bowl of a food processor. Using the metal blade, process until fine crumbs form. Pour into a small bowl and set aside.

2. Preheat the oven to 400°F. Generously butter two baking sheets (or more if you have them). In a medium bowl, using an electric mixer, beat the butter for about 1 minute, until creamy. Add the remaining sugar and beat for about 1 minute, until light and fluffy. Gradually beat in the egg whites and almond extract until well blended. Sift over the already sifted flour and fold into the butter mixture, then fold in the reserved almond-sugar mixture.

3. Begin by working in batches of 4 cookies on each sheet. Drop tablespoonfuls of batter about 6 inches apart onto a baking sheet. Using the back of a moistened spoon, spread each mound of batter into very thin 3-inch rounds. Each round should be transparent. It does not matter if you make a few holes—the batter will spread evenly and fill them in. Sprinkle the tops with some flaked almonds.

4. Bake, one sheet at a time, for 4–5 minutes, until the cookie edges are lightly browned and the centers are just golden. Remove the baking sheet to a wire rack and, working quickly, use a thin-bladed metal spatula to loosen the edge of a hot cookie. Transfer to a rolling pin or glass tumbler and gently press the sides down. Repeat with the remaining cookie rounds.

A color illustration from a recipe pamphlet published in 1934 by Church & Dwight Co.

This wonderful Chef cookie jar was made by The Regal China Company. It began making jars in 1938 and finally went out of business in 1992.

5. If the cookies become too firm to transfer from the baking sheet, return the sheet to the oven for 30 seconds to soften the cookie dough, then proceed as above. Continue baking and shaping with the remaining dough. When cool, transfer the cookies immediately to airtight containers in single layers. These cookies are very fragile.

Chocolate Cream Brandy Snaps

Makes about 2½ dozen cookies

COOKIES

Butter and/or vegetable oil, for greasing

½ cup (1 stick) unsalted butter, cut into pieces

2 tablespoons corn syrup

¼ cup sugar

¼ cup packed light brown sugar

1 teaspoon ground ginger

2 tablespoons brandy

½ cup all-purpose flour

CHOCOLATE WHIPPED CREAMS

1¼ cups whipping cream

½ teaspoon vanilla extract

2 ounces bittersweet or semisweet chocolate, melted

2 ounces white chocolate, melted

1. Preheat the oven to 350°F. Generously butter or oil two large baking sheets (or more if you have them), or use nonstick baking sheets. Lightly oil two wooden spoon handles. In a heavy-based saucepan over medium heat, bring to a boil the butter, corn syrup, sugars, and ginger, stirring constantly until the sugars dissolve. Remove from the heat and stir in the brandy and flour until well blended and smooth. Place the pan in a shallow bowl of hot water.

A wire-handled cake or mixing spoon, dating from around the 1910 to 1920s era.

2. Begin by working in batches of no more than 4 cookies on each sheet. Drop tablespoonfuls of batter about 6 inches apart onto the baking sheet. Using the back of a moistened spoon, spread each mound into about 3-inch rounds (the cookies will spread further). Bake for 7–10 minutes, until golden and bubbling, turning the baking sheet if the cookies brown unevenly.

3. Remove the baking sheet to a wire rack and cool for about 1 minute. Working quickly, use a thin-bladed metal spatula to loosen the edge of a hot cookie and lift it from the sheet. Roll the cookie around the oiled handle of one of the wooden spoons, pressing down on the seam for a few seconds. Repeat with another cookie; you can fit 2 cookies per spoon, or do them one at a time.

4. Slide the cookies off the spoon handles and place on a wire rack to cool completely. Repeat with the remaining cookies. If they become too brittle to roll, return the baking sheet to the oven for 30 seconds to soften. The cookies should be flexible but firm enough to lift off without wrinkling and tearing. Repeat with remaining batter.

5. Up to 2 hours before serving, in a large bowl, using an electric mixer, beat the cream and vanilla extract until stiff peaks form. Quickly fold half the cream into the melted bittersweet or semisweet chocolate until completely blended. Fold the remaining cream into the melted white chocolate. Spoon the dark chocolate cream into a medium pastry bag fitted with a medium star tip. Pipe cream into both ends of half the cookies and place on a baking sheet. Spoon the white chocolate cream into another pastry bag fitted with a medium star tip and pipe into both ends of the remaining cookies. Refrigerate until ready to serve. Do not fill too early or the moisture will soften the brandy snaps. Arrange on a plate to serve. Store unfilled cookies in airtight containers with waxed paper between the layers.

Raspberry Rugelach

Makes about 5½ dozen cookies

THIS TRADITIONAL JEWISH-AMERICAN COOKIE IS MADE WITH A TENDER CREAM CHEESE PASTRY.

2 cups all-purpose flour

½ teaspoon salt

½ cup (1 stick) unsalted butter, softened

4 ounces cream cheese, softened

¼ cup sour cream

3 tablespoons superfine sugar

1 egg, separated

Vegetable oil spray or vegetable oil, for greasing

1 cup seedless raspberry preserves

½ cup mini white chocolate chips or 3 ounces chopped semisweet chocolate

¼ cup finely chopped, unblanched almonds

¼ cup sugar

1. Sift the flour and salt into a bowl. In another bowl, using an electric mixer, beat the butter, cream cheese, sour cream, sugar, and the egg yolk until creamy and smooth. Stir in the flour until a soft dough forms and holds together. Knead lightly to blend. Shape the dough into a ball and flatten to a disc. Wrap tightly and refrigerate for 1–2 hours, until firm enough to handle.

2. Preheat the oven to 350°F. Lightly spray or grease 2 large baking sheets. On a lightly floured surface, using a floured rolling pin, roll one-quarter of the dough ⅛-inch thick. Refrigerate the remaining dough. Using a 10- to 11-inch diameter plate as a guide, cut the dough into a 10–11-inch round. Spread the round with about 3 tablespoons of raspberry preserves to within ½ inch of the edge of the dough. Sprinkle with a few chocolate chips.

3. Cut the dough round into 12 equal wedges. Starting at the curved edge, roll up each wedge jelly-roll fashion to resemble a croissant. Place the cookies point side down 1½ inches apart on one of the baking sheets. In a small bowl, beat the egg white with 1 tablespoon of water and brush each cookie with a little of the glaze. Sprinkle each cookie with chopped almonds and a little sugar.

4. Bake for 20–25 minutes, until puffed and golden brown, rotating the cookie sheet from front to back halfway through the cooking time. Remove the baking sheet to a wire rack and, using a thin-bladed metal spatula, remove the cookies to a wire rack to cool. Repeat with the remaining dough and trimmings. Store in airtight containers with waxed paper between each layer.

Florentines

Makes about 30 cookies

FLORENTINES ARE AN ITALIAN-STYLE COOKIE, MADE FROM A BATTER-TYPE DOUGH. THEY ARE FILLED WITH CANDIED PEEL AND COATED WITH CHOCOLATE ON ONE SIDE.

Vegetable oil spray or vegetable oil, for greasing
½ cup heavy cream
¼ cup (½ stick) butter
½ cup superfine sugar
2 tablespoons honey
1⅓ cups slivered almonds
5 tablespoons all-purpose flour

Grated zest of 1 orange
¾ teaspoon ground cinnamon
½ cup diced candied orange peel
½ cup diced candied citron (lemon peel)
½ cup diced candied cherries
4 ounces semisweet chocolate, melted
4 ounces white chocolate, melted

1. Preheat the oven to 350°F. Lightly spray or grease 2 large, nonstick baking sheets. In a medium saucepan over low heat, stir the cream, butter, sugar, and honey until the sugar is dissolved. Increase the heat to high and bring the mixture to a boil, stirring constantly. Remove the pan from the heat and stir in the almonds, flour, orange zest, and ground cinnamon until well blended, then stir in the diced candied fruits.

2. Drop the mixture by teaspoonfuls at least 3 inches apart onto the baking sheets. Using the back of a moistened spoon, carefully spread each circle as thinly as possible.

3. Bake for 8–10 minutes, until the edges are golden and the cookies are bubbling. Do not overbake since the cookies can burn easily, but do not underbake or the cookies will be too sticky to handle. Remove the baking sheets to wire racks and cool slightly. For perfectly round cookies, use a 3–4-inch round cookie cutter to cut round the edges while the cookies are still hot on the baking sheet. Cool slightly until just set. Using a thin-bladed metal spatula, remove the cookies to wire racks to cool completely.

4. When completely cooled, spread half the cookies with the melted semisweet chocolate on the flat side of each cookie and place chocolate side up on wire racks. Spread the remaining cookies with the melted white chocolate. Refrigerate for 2–3 minutes, until the chocolate is just setting. If you like, using a serrated knife or 4-tined fork, make wavy lines on the chocolate layer. Refrigerate for 10–15 minutes to set completely. Store in the refrigerator in airtight containers with waxed paper between the layers.

A charming, festive cookie jar for storing those special Christmas favorites, featuring the enduring Mickey and Minnie Mouse.

Fried Bow-Ties

Makes about 6 dozen cookies

TRADITIONAL IN MANY COUNTRIES SUCH AS MEXICO, ITALY, SPAIN, AND THE MIDDLE EAST, THESE COOKIES ARE FRIED NOT BOILED.

3 eggs
¼ cup milk
¼ cup sugar
½ teaspoon salt
2 teaspoons vanilla extract

2¼ cups all-purpose flour
Vegetable oil, for frying
Confectioner's sugar, for dusting

1. In a large bowl, using an electric mixer, beat the eggs, milk, sugar, salt, and vanilla extract until blended. On low speed, beat in 1½ cups of the flour, then stir in the remaining flour to form a soft dough. Scrape the dough onto a sheet of plastic wrap or waxed paper and flatten to a disc shape. Refrigerate for 2–3 hours, until firm.

2. On a lightly floured surface, using a floured rolling pin, roll out half the dough, as thinly as possible, ⅛-inch thick or thinner. Cut the dough into 4 x 1½-inch strips. With a sharp knife, cut a l-inch lengthwise slit in the center of each strip. Carefully pull one end of the rectangle through the center slit, and pull through to form the bow-tie shape. Continue with the remaining dough.

3. In a deep-fat fryer or deep-sided, heavy frying pan, heat about 2 inches of oil to 350°F on a deep-fat thermometer. Carefully drop in a few bow-ties at a time and fry for about 1½ minutes, until golden. With a slotted metal pancake turner or spoon, remove to a double thickness of paper towels to drain. Cool completely, then dust with confectioner's sugar. Best eaten the same day.

Lemon Pizzelles

Makes about 3 dozen wedges

1¾ cups all-purpose flour
2 teaspoons baking powder
½ teaspoon salt
3 eggs, lightly beaten
¾ cup sugar

½ cup (1 stick) unsalted butter, melted
Grated zest of 1 lemon
1 tablespoon lemon extract
Confectioner's sugar, for dusting

1. Preheat a 7-inch electric pizzelle or other waffle iron as the manufacturer directs. Sift the flour, baking powder, and salt into a large bowl.

2. Make a well in the center of the flour mixture and pour in the eggs, sugar, melted butter, lemon zest, and lemon extract. Using an electric mixer on low speed, beat the liquid ingredients until blended, then slowly incorporate the flour from the edge of the well until all the mixture is smooth. Thin with a little milk or water if necessary.

3. Using a small ladle, pour about 2 tablespoons of batter into the center of the pizzelle or waffle iron. Pull down the cover and allow to bake, without lifting the cover, for the time specified by the pizzelle or waffle iron manufacturer.

4. Lift the cover and use a thin-bladed metal spatula or fork to lift the edge of the cookie. Slide onto a wire rack to cool completely. Repeat with the remaining batter. Dust with confectioner's sugar and store in airtight containers. Alternatively, keep the pizzelles warm in an oven heated to 250°F while baking, and serve the cookies warm, dusted with confectioner's sugar and dipped in a little jam or maple syrup.

Coconut Fortune Cookies

Makes about 4 dozen cookies

THESE CHINESE-STYLE FORTUNE COOKIES ARE SO MUCH FUN TO MAKE AND DELICIOUS TOO! THEY MAKE A GREAT SIMPLE DESSERT AFTER AN ORIENTAL-STYLE MEAL.

Vegetable oil, for greasing

All-purpose flour

2 egg whites

⅓ cup confectioner's sugar, sifted

1 teaspoon coconut or almond extract

2 tablespoons unsalted butter, melted

⅓ cup cake flour, sifted

¼ cup sweetened shredded coconut, toasted and chopped

1. Grease and flour 2 large baking sheets (or more if you have them). Using a round cookie cutter, glass, or ramekin 3 inches in diameter, mark 2 circles in diagonal corners of each baking sheet (the cookies will spread).

2. In a medium bowl, using an electric mixer, beat the egg whites until foamy. Gradually beat in the confectioner's sugar, coconut or almond extract, and melted butter. On low speed, beat in the flour until well blended and smooth.

3. Heat the oven to 350°F. Drop a level teaspoon of batter in the centers of each marked circle on the baking sheets. Using the back of a

moistened spoon, spread the batter evenly to cover the circles completely. Sprinkle each circle with toasted coconut.

4. Bake, one sheet at a time, for about 5 minutes, until the cookie edges are lightly browned. Remove the baking sheet to a wire rack and, working quickly, use a thin-bladed metal spatula to loosen the edge of a cookie. Set on a board, fold in half, and with the fold facing upward, bend each cookie over the rim of a glass, creating the classic shape. Hold for 30 seconds. Place on a wire rack to cool.

5. Repeat with the remaining cookies. If the cookies become too crisp to remove and shape, return to the oven for 30 seconds to soften. Repeat with the remaining batter and coconut. When cool, store in airtight containers with waxed paper between the layers.

Index

A

Almond and Ginger Biscotti 32
almond cookies 26, 32, 40, 53, 58, 63, 72, 76
Almond-Meringue Cream Sandwiches 58
Amaretti, Chocolate 53

B

baking cookies 12–13
bar cookies 60–69
Butterscotch Bars with Meringue Topping 67

C

Chewy Caramel Nut Squares 66
Chocolate Amaretti 53
chocolate cookies 16, 19, 22, 27, 28, 38, 47, 52, 53, 55, 62, 63, 74,
Chocolate Cream Brandy Snaps 74
Chocolate-Dipped Hazelnut Crescents 28
Chocolate-Dipped Lime Ribbons 52
Chocolate Nut Crackles 22
Chocolate-Pecan Brownies 62
Chocolate Pistachio Pinwheels 47
Chocolate Raspberry Macaroon Bars 63
Chocolate Turtles 20
Chocolate Viennese Fingers 55
Christmas Cut-out Cookies 48
Coconut Fortune Cookies 79
Coconut Lime Squares 39
Coconut Macaroons 23
Cookie Jar Gingersnaps 30
Cream Cheese Macadamia Drops with White Chocolate 19

D

Date-Filled Oat Crumb Squares 65
Death by Chocolate 16
drop cookies 14-35

F

Florentines 76
French Almond Tile Cookies 72
Fried Bow-Ties 78
Fruit 'n' Nut Oatmeal Cookies 17

G

ginger cookies 30, 32, 38, 44
Gingery Chocolate Cookies 38

H

hazelnut cookies 28, 43
Hazelnut Marmalade Swirls 43
Honey and Lemon Madeleines 30

L

Lacy Oatmeal Wafers 23
Lemon Bars 64
Lemon Pizzelles 78

M

macaroons 23, 26
Mexican Wedding Cakes 31
molded cookies 24–35
Moravian Spice Squares 46

N

New Wave Peanut Butter Cookies 18
nut cookies 16, 17, 18, 20, 22, 23, 26, 27, 28, 31, 32, 40, 42, 43, 47, 52, 53, 58, 62, 63, 65, 66, 72, 76

P

Peanut Butter Cookie-Cups 27
peanut butter cookies 18, 27
Peppermint Cookie Canes 34
Pine Nut Macaroons 26
Poppy Seed Spirals 42
pressed and piped cookies 50–59

R

Raspberry Jam Sandwiches 40
Raspberry Rugelach 75

refrigerated and rolled cookies 36–49

S

Scottish Shortbread 68
Shrewsbury Biscuits 46
special cookies 70–79
spice cookies 30, 32, 44, 46, 54
Spicy Gingerbread Cactus 44
Spiral Spice Cookies 54
Spritz Cookies 56
Strawberry Thumbprints 57

W

white chocolate cookies 18, 19, 75, 76

Acknowledgments

The publishers wish to thank the following collectors, organisations, and picture libraries who have supplied the photographs (and/or items for photography) that are featured in the book. Photographs have been credited by page number and position on the page: (B) Bottom, (T) Top, (C) Centre, (BL) Bottom left, (BR) Bottom right, (TL) Top left, (TR) Top right.

Phoebe Phillips: pages 6 (T), 7 (BL).

New York Public Library: pages 4 (BL), 5 (TR), 6 (BR).

Johnson & Wales University Culinary Archives & Museum: pages 4 (BR), 7 (TR, BR); 8, 9, 10, 11, 14–15, 20 (BL), 28 (BL), 32, 34 (BL), 36–37, 39, 42, 47, 52, 53, 54, 57, 58 (TR), 63 (TR), 64 (TR), 67 (TR), 68 (BL), 72 (BL), 74, 76 (BL), 79.
Louise Messina Daking and Geoff Daking: jacket; pages 1, 4 (TL and BR), 5 (BL), 12–13, 17, 19, 20 (TR), 23, 28 (TR), 34 (TR), 40, 43, 44, 48, 55, 58 (BL), 66 (BL), 68 (TR), 72 (TR), 76 (BR).

Kravette Jericho, New York: endpapers, pages 2, 18.

The National Magazine Company: 50–51, 60-61.

Mary Evans Picture Library: 70–71.